Twayne's United States Authors Series

Sylvia E. Bowman, *Editor*

INDIANA UNIVERSITY

Timothy Flint

TIMOTHY FLINT

By JAMES K. FOLSOM

Yale University

Twayne Publishers, Inc. :: New York

818.2
F625

To Q. K. F.

SCHOLAR, GENTLEMAN, FRIEND

Preface

IN THE INTRODUCTION to his 1911 biography of Timothy Flint, John Ervin Kirkpatrick rather gloomily remarked that among the professors of his acquaintance at Yale only one knew anything of Flint and his work. My own admittedly incomplete researches into Flint's mid-twentieth-century reputation give some reason for cautious optimism; for in the same institution I have turned up two professors and a graduate student whose knowledge of Flint's life and work is more than casual. Yet no one would pretend that Flint is a runaway popular success with either the scholarly or the undergraduate audience, nor has the lack of a full-length study of his work seemed, up to now, a major flaw in American criticism. The reader of this study may then very properly ask, before beginning it, why it exists in the first place. What reason is there to resurrect so minor a figure in the pantheon of American letters?

Two answers come immediately to mind. The first, and less compelling, is a historical one. However little Flint's work is prized now, at the time he was writing readers thought highly of it. If to us it seems sadly dated and almost devoid of interest, the question of why it was originally so much esteemed becomes all the more challenging. One purpose of this study therefore will be to attempt an investigation of the nature of Flint's contemporary reputation.

More important than the historical justification for this study, however, is a polemical one. For in my opinion Kirkpatrick was right in suggesting that Flint's writing has been unjustly forgotten. Though I do not intend in this essay to be pointlessly vehement in hopes of seating Flint beside Hawthorne or Melville or Henry James, yet I think it possible to argue reasonably that present-day neglect *in toto* of Flint's work is as misguided as was the too-great adulation given him over a century ago.

It is noteworthy that of all the many students of Flint almost none has dealt with the literary value of his work. They have examined his biography; deplored his regrettably short temper; defended his reputation against calumnies of various kinds; admired his religious, political, social, and economic opinions; and traced his influence upon other writers. But somehow his work itself has never been considered of sufficient importance to warrant any more than cursory critical study. As a result, the modern oblivion to which Flint is consigned can scarcely be said to be a consequence of that reasoned scholarly opinion which, having judiciously considered all the evidence at hand, has decided that his writing is abysmally bad—and the less said about it the better.

The focus of this study, then, will be primarily literary. In it will be found only a survey biography, admittedly slanted toward an exposition of Flint's literary career: whether or not he treated Mrs. Trollope unjustly, what were the rights and wrongs of his quarrel with the editor of the *Athenaeum,* and whether his opinions of Robert Owen were sensible or not form no part of this essay. Neither do his religious opinions, except as they influence his fictional craft, come in for praise or blame. With Flint himself I am not concerned; many able scholars have investigated his biography, and while I have drawn liberally on their researches, I have not written another and to my mind superfluous biographical account. With his work I am concerned; to the best of my knowledge this study is the first to attempt an assessment of its literary merit, indicating what is of interest and value to the modern reader. My approach has been subjective: some of Flint's works I find much more impressive than others, and I have not attempted to conceal my own value judgments behind a mask of objectivity. I have, however, given all Flint's work a careful reading and, to the best of my ability, a sympathetic critical evaluation.

A few individual stylistic vagaries should be pointed out. I have dispensed with footnotes wherever possible, incorporating page references into the text; and I have often abbreviated citations to quotations from Flint's writing which I have used only in passing or by way of example. All references are fully documented in the bibliography, and what few unfamiliar abbreviations may occur in the notes have been expanded there. I have also quoted at some—perhaps too-great—length from Flint's writing, rather than paraphrasing his quotations. I have

Preface

assumed that the reader's familiarity with Flint's work is not
extensive, and that consequently he would welcome the inter-
polation of passages from the books under discussion so that
he might make up his own mind about their stylistic merit.
Flint's punctuation, which does not always accord with twentieth-
century practice, I have left untouched; nor have I changed
his spelling when, on occasion, it varies from the modern. In a
few places I have added, in brackets, an explanatory note to
clarify what I thought was a doubtful point.

I am happy here to record my obligation to those who have
helped in the preparation of this study. Special thanks are due
to Mrs. Anne Whelpley, Assistant Librarian of the Yale Collection
of American Literature, and to Mr. Archibald Hanna, Jr.,
Curator of the Yale Western Americana Collection; to Professor
William H. Goetzmann; and to Mr. Nolan Smith, whose own
research turned up many hitherto unknown nineteenth-century
reviews of Flint. To my wife many thanks for moral support
in general and for superhuman patience in particular while
reading the first drafts of this manuscript; and to Q. K. F. who
suffered patiently while the book was being written.

James K. Folsom

Yale University
New Haven, Connecticut

Contents

Chronology

1780   Timothy Flint born, North Reading, Massachusetts, probably on July 11.

1795   Phillips Academy, Andover, Massachusetts.

1796-1800   Harvard. Graduates, Bachelor of Arts, 1800.

1801   Teaches in academy at Cohasset, Massachusetts, and preaches at Marblehead. Continues study of theology.

1802   Marries Abigail Hubbard at Marblehead. Ordained.

1802-1814   Pastor of the Church at Lunenburg, Massachusetts.

1814   Resigns pastorate at Lunenburg; missionary work in New Hampshire.

1815   Missionary work in Massachusetts and in New York; moves West; settles at Cincinnati.

1815-1816   Missionary work in Ohio, Indiana, and Kentucky under the auspices of the Missionary Society of Connecticut.

1816   Moves to St. Louis, and later to St. Charles, Missouri; meets Daniel Boone; missionary work in Missouri.

1818   Resigns from Missionary Society of Connecticut.

1819   Failing health forces journey south to Arkansas; returns to New Madrid, Missouri, by December.

1820   To Jackson, Missouri.

1821   Returns to St. Charles; entire family ill; decides to farm.

1822   Goes south again, to New Orleans, intending to return to New England.

1823   Settles in Alexandria, Louisiana; teaches; declining health.

1825   To Salem, Massachusetts; September, 1825, returns to Alexandria.

1826   Another trip to New England. *Recollections of the Last Ten Years* and *Francis Berrian* published.

1827-   Returns to Cincinnati. Edits (1827-30) *Western Monthly*
1833   *Review*. Period of greatest literary productivity. *A Condensed Geography and History of the Western States* (1828), *Arthur Clenning* (1828), *George Mason* (1829), *The Lost Child* (1830), *The Shoshonee Valley* (1830), *The Personal Narrative of James O. Pattie* (1831), *The Art of Being Happy* (1832), *The History and Geography of the Mississippi Valley* (1832), *Indian Wars of the West* (1833), *Biographical Memoir of Daniel Boone* (1833), *Lectures Upon Natural History* (1833).

1833   Failing health forces journey to New England and New York. Accepts position as editor of *The Knickerbocker* (1833), which he soon resigns because of ill health. Apparently edits only one issue (October, 1833), but continues to contribute articles and fiction until 1836.

1834   Returns to Alexandria. *The Bachelor Reclaimed.*

1834-   Failing health forces various long journeys for conva-
1839   lescence. Visits New England, Cuba, Canada.

1840   Final trip to New England. Dies, August 16, 1840, in North Reading, Massachusetts. Buried August 20 in Salem.

Timothy Flint

CHAPTER *1*

Life

TIMOTHY FLINT'S two most perceptive and sympathetic biographers have seized upon one fact of his life as being of the first importance. For William H. Venable, Flint was "missionary, geographer, editor, novelist, and poet," and for John E. Kirkpatrick he was "pioneer, missionary, author, editor."[1] In the titles of their two separate biographies, both authors have indicated the variety of Flint's life as its single most important fact; and though neither biographer has chosen to discuss Flint's work as somehow typical of his life, yet each has realized that Flint's biography is in some way emblematic of a larger order of American experience. However ludicrously the long subtitles of these two biographies may strike us, they would not have struck Flint's contemporaries so; for they show that Flint was, in his own way, squarely in the main current of early nineteenth-century American life, a life which was lived by grasping whatever opportunity was at hand and, when one opportunity proved disappointing, by seizing another. If these subtitles indicate to us that Flint was a Jack-of-all-trades, Flint's contemporaries would have been only too approving; and if we point out that a Jack-of-all-trades is proverbially a master of none, the attitude is ours, and not theirs. What of Washington, Flint's contemporaries would ask—surveyor, soldier, farmer, and statesman? Or of Jefferson—farmer, philosopher, scientist, author, educator, and patriot?

In sum, Flint's biography is typical, in a sense, not only of all American biography in the early years of the Republic, but of one class of American biography in particular—that of the pioneer. And his contemporaries would have recognized it as such. Living before Frederick Jackson Turner, whose discussion in 1893 of the significance of the American frontier wrought a revolution both in American historiography and in American myth-history, Flint's contemporaries, by and large, did not see the frontiersman as the romantic figure which he later became to the American imagination. They were more inclined to discover in him a very rough diamond indeed, necessary perhaps in a providential scheme of things to stop Indian bullets which might otherwise bring down a more worth-while member of society, but otherwise not the sort of person one would really want to know. With Crèvecoeur, writing in 1782, they would have agreed that "remote from the power of example, and check of shame," the frontiersmen "exhibit the most hideous parts of our society. They are a kind of forlorn hope."[2] Or, as Flint himself put it, in discussing the mountain men, those paragons of Western virtue from across the wide Missouri, "They furnish an impressive proof, that there is no mode of life intrinsically so repulsive and painful, but man may become reconciled to it by habit."[3] No, the frontiersmen were not the heroes of the saga of America. They were needed to clear the way, but the heroic work would be done, to continue Crèvecoeur's quotation, by that "most respectable army of veterans which come after them," who "will change in a few years that hitherto barbarous country into a fine fertile, well regulated district."

It is as one of those respectable veterans that Timothy Flint is of biographical importance. For to Flint's contemporaries, the man who came after the frontiersman, and not the frontiersman himself was the real hero of the American experience. The Daniel Boones, the James Harrods, the Jim Bridgers were merely shock troops to prepare the way for the triumph of Columbia and the civilizing of its barbarous inhabitants. Like all shock troops, they were expendable; and, though their history might prove of passing interest, their significance was to be seen in terms of the total campaign. For Washington Irving, writing in *Astoria* the history of the campaign to establish the American fur trade on the Pacific Coast, the mountain men are indeed visualized as a kind of cannon fodder. When not downright traitorous they are at best amiable buffoons, and the hero of *Astoria* is their general, John Jacob Astor, whose motives, according to Irving, are not sordid ones of gain, but patriotic ones of conquest.[4] For the frontiersman, to Flint's contemporaries, was not the melancholy last man of a noble race so much as the forerunner of a new and happier society. His rewards came from the contemplation of the world he had made safe for democracy; and, when he looked around him, he proudly observed that "where wretched wigwams stood, the miserable abodes of savages, we behold the foundations of cities laid, that, in all probability, will rival the glory of the greatest upon earth."[5] It is with the inhabitants of these cities, not with their founders, that Timothy Flint's contemporaries concerned themselves.

I *Early Life*

Timothy Flint was born in 1780 in North Reading, Massachusetts, probably on July 11, though the first authenticated report of him is his baptismal record of July 23. His parents, William and Martha Kimball Flint, were descendants of old New England stock. The Flints had come from England to Salem, Massachusetts, about 1638, and had never moved far away, though Timothy's great-grandfather (also named William) had settled in North Reading about 1700. The North Reading homestead where young Timothy was born was the property of the Flint family from about 1700 until 1828, when Timothy's father died.

Timothy was the fifth of nine children, and apparently even as a child was not very robust. He was sent early to school, and spent a good part of his school days in Salem with relatives. His father was a yeoman, but Timothy, whether because of illness or of congenital unwillingness to engage in farm work, seems to have done little on the family farm. Later in Missouri he was to attempt, with disastrous results, farming for a livelihood—a life which, it is more than likely, he would never have tried had he had as a child more vivid firsthand acquaintance with its rigors.

In 1787, before Timothy's eighth birthday, his uncle, Hezekiah Flint, left New England for the new Western settlement of "Marietta on the Ohio." Timothy remembered this event clearly enough to recall in mature life the black canvas that covered the wagon, with "To Marietta on the Ohio" written on it in large white letters.[6] Despite the prophecies of the certain failure of the colonization experiment, Uncle Hezekiah never returned from the West, though he moved from Marietta to Cincinnati, where he died in 1811. His son, also named Hezekiah, was one of the leading citizens of Cincinnati, and his presence there—he lived until 1843—was doubtless one of the factors which determined Timothy's later decision to settle in that city.

The particulars of Timothy's youthful life are unknown except in general outline. We know that in 1795 he was enrolled at Phillips Academy in Andover, Massachusetts; but it is unlikely that he spent more time there than one year. His schooling was probably directed by the minister of the North Reading church, the Reverend Eliab Stone, and by David Everett, a Dartmouth graduate who taught school in North Reading. Micah, the son of the Reverend Stone, was a tutor at Harvard College where Timothy studied from 1796 to 1800; and it is likely that Timothy's own son Micah was named for him. Of Flint's college years we know almost nothing. Apparently his life there was happy, and he, along with his cousin James Flint, who was two years behind him at Harvard, decided to study for the ministry.

By the time of his graduation from Harvard, Flint's commitment to the ministry was, for the time being at least, certain. After graduation he taught for one year in an academy at Cohasset and preached at Marblehead. His cousin, the Reverend Jacob Flint, an older brother of James, was pastor of the Cohasset church, and Flint probably continued his theological studies under Jacob's direction. While preaching at Marblehead, Timothy met and married, on July 12, 1802, Abigail Hubbard, five years his junior and the daughter of the Reverend Ebenezer Hubbard. In 1802, before his twenty-second birthday, he was called to the pulpit of the parish of Lunenburg, forty miles from Boston.

The circumstances of Timothy's entire early life seem to have brought him inevitably to the pulpit. As a boy he was under the influence of ministerial teaching, he graduated from Harvard when a Harvard education usually, if not invariably, led to the ministry, and he married into a ministerial family. His closest friend, his cousin James, also became a minister. Yet Flint himself, though occasionally an itinerant preacher and always an ostentatiously godly man, was soon to become disillusioned with the ministry, to give up his pastorate after twelve years, and four years later, his official ministerial connection with the church. From 1818 on he would preach only as an itinerant or as a guest minister.

The ostensible reasons for this change of heart are to be found in his inability and unwillingness to cope with the temporizing principles of ecclesiastical politics. Kirkpatrick, in his biography of Flint, strongly implies that Flint was a man somehow too good for this world, unable and unwilling to compromise with principle, and this view has been the general one of Flint's biographers. The ministry, according to this general biographical interpretation, was basic to Flint's life; and all the rest of his activities were dependent upon this ministerial bias. Yet on the basis of the evidence it seems to me that a different interpretation is nearer the truth. One does not get an overwhelming impression from Flint's writing that he was a man with a real call to the saving of souls, but rather that appurtenances of the clerical life attracted him. The satisfactions he wished to gain from the ministry, one feels, were not those of pastoral service, but rather the general satisfactions of the contemplative life—of study, of reflection, and of literature. It is to be noted that his religious mentors were scholars as well and that his cousin James in particular was later to be the inspiration for his career as an author.

But in 1802 this was all in the future, and Timothy accepted the call to the pastorate of Lunenburg.

II *The Pastorate of Lunenburg*

Before giving a call to a minister, it was customary in the early years of the nineteenth century to invite him to preach, so that the congregation might know what to expect. Accordingly, the congregation at Lunenburg invited Flint to preach for four Sundays, from April 18 to May 9, 1802, in order that it might evaluate his capabilities. After four Sundays the congregation was still apparently unable to make up its mind; it asked him to preach another Sunday, after which it gave him a formal call. But a long squabble over salary—prophetic of the future—interrupted the negotiations so that it was not until the sixth of October that Flint was actually ordained. The final arrangement gave Flint $1,000 for his settlement and an annual salary of $400. In addition, to commemorate the call, the pulpit of the Lunenburg church was redecorated and the galleries renovated at a cost of $100.

The ordination was a large and grand occasion. The Reverend Eliab Stone preached the ordination sermon, and the Reverend Jacob Flint of Cohasset was invited to attend. All in all, it was an auspicious beginning for a new, young, and ambitious minister. But it was not long before whatever good will there had been between the pastor and his flock began to evaporate. Reasons for the growing coolness are hard to assign, but they seem to have been basically attributable to a lack of tact on the part of the young minister, whose ways caused a certain amount of consternation among the good people of Lunenburg. For one thing, in a time of bitter party feeling, Flint was a Federalist in a predominantly Democratic parish. Some of the patriots in the town felt that he was downright disloyal, and one even brought the charge of counterfeiting against their pastor, an accusation which Flint felt to be so serious that he prosecuted and won damages. But it was probably a Pyrrhic victory, for the charge does not seem really to have been counterfeiting so much as incompatibility.

Added to his suspicious politics was the fact that Flint's religious principles were perhaps questionable. For one thing he was scandalously lax in sound Calvinist maxims, and the doctrine of his sermons might well have caused a strict believer to worry. In a schismatic age he preached the doctrine that sectarianism was an unqualified evil—and what is worse, he preached it untactfully. Much later, on a return journey to New England, Flint was to describe the results of a foolish insistence on small points of dogma:

> It was painful to learn, that the people were so divided into schisms, and had formed so many churches, that no one possessed the means of sustaining a regular worship. There were the two or three churches, erected as hostile spiritual batteries against each other, where the means of the whole place were with difficulty adequate to the support of a single minister. In the whole excursion, from the green hills of the interior of New-Hampshire to the limit of a sea board ride on the south shore, in

almost every village we saw this same array of rival churches, where the population called for but one. We every where heard the bickering and tale bearing of mutual efforts at proselytism.[7]

By 1833 he had learned the proper note. This reproof, tempered with the wisdom of a man of fifty-three, is elegiac, mournful, and—though pointed in application—not specific in allusion. It is the kind of reproof Americans love: it is properly melancholy in feeling without being unpleasantly personal. In 1826, however, twelve years after his separation from the church at Lunenburg, Flint had not been quite so moderate. Speaking of Ohio, he observes that "it is generally denominated in the western country the Yankee state," because of its closeness to Yankee ways, among which are the "disposition [on the part of its inhabitants] to dogmatize, to settle, not only their own faith, but that of their neighbour, and to stand resolutely, and dispute fiercely, for the slightest shade of difference of religious opinion."[8]

And in 1808—while he was still pastor of the church at Lunenburg—he had uttered even more trenchant views. In a sermon preached at the ordination of his brother-in-law, Flint gave full sway to the anti-theological cast of his thought. Speaking to the fledgling minister about the most effective means for the conversion of sinners, he remarked that, though the agent of conversion must be a good man in order to be effective, yet the instruments of conversion should be Gospel exhortations rather than reason and morality. Moreover, the failure to convert is apparently largely due to the minister's reliance on methods other than exhortation. "It is melancholy to consider how many," he says pointedly, "rejecting the simplicity and energy of gospel motives, have exhausted their strength in dispensing, not the substantial food, which can alone rear the sinner up to the maturity and stature of a man in *Christ Jesus our Lord,* but in dispensing the *east wind,* the idle efforts of their own talents and invention." Not only that, but "it is questionable, whether it be Christian policy to be perpetually engaged in combating infidelity, among professed believers, and to occupy more time in detailing the defence of an undescribed religion, than in teaching what religion is, and the indispensable necessity of that religion to sinners."[9]

In this sermon Flint is skating on some pretty thin theological ice. No one, not even the most hidebound parishioner, would deny the efficacy of Gospel exhortation in conversion. Yet, he might ask, because exhortation on occasion proves effective, does this mean that all other means should be abandoned? What of the man with religious doubts, or with some peculiar biblical interpretation of his own? What of the Unitarians, for instance, especially since the Reverend James Flint had recently become one? Is not the only way to convert them by reason? It is all very well to talk about the brotherhood of Man and the fatherhood of God, but don't specific differences of opinion have to be decided by an appeal to reason?

In short, Flint's religious orientation was evangelical, non-theological, while his parish was probably orthodoxly Calvinist, brought up within the strong Calvinistic tradition of rational disputation. It is not beside the point to note here that Flint in his later writings always speaks well of camp meetings; of the impressiveness of the spectacle; and, more to the point of the present discussion, of the effectiveness of that rude but forceful preaching which comes, we trust, from the heart. Similarly, he remains throughout his life a student of the various styles of pulpit oratory. Though he often ridicules the barbarousness of delivery of uneducated Western ministers, yet he is at the same time sympathetic to their forceful expression, which he almost invariably contrasts favorably to the dry intellectualism of the New England clergy.

Though Flint himself would have been the first to deny it, his own religious persuasion was very close to what William James was later to dub "nothingarian." Religious belief for Flint was more or less equivalent to moral action. A religious man was a "good" man for him, and he never attempted to go behind this rather simple-minded equation. As a result we look in vain in all his writings for any habit of thought which in any traditional rationalistic sense can properly be called either "theological" or "philosophical." He believes in a conventional piety without—unlike his Calvinist forebears—ever really attempting to assess its basis; similarly, though he believes in a certain common-sense practicality of action, he does not anticipate in any technical way the beliefs of the later Pragmatists. Exhortation to goodness by means of biblical—and to a lesser degree historical—example is Flint's ultimate religious concern.

It is, of course, dangerous to generalize too far about Flint's religious differences with his congregation, chiefly because the evidence is so sparse. Yet even had Flint been soundly orthodox, his behavior would have caused some talk in Lunenburg. The silliest of the many causes of trouble in the parish centered around a laboratory which Flint had built and where he dabbled in chemistry. Some of his parishioners seem to have thought that chemistry was a branch of the black art and that the minister's devotion to it was sinful.

The most interesting thing about this charge is that it would never have arisen had Flint had anything approaching decent relations with his parishioners. Yet he apparently never made any attempt to conciliate public opinion or, indeed, even to observe the amenities of normal social intercourse. The story is told, for example, that when a young man of Lunenburg who had the reputation of being a reprobate died, Flint preached a funeral sermon beginning with the hymn

> My thoughts on awful subjects roll,
> Damnation, and the dead.

This quality of what Kirkpatrick calls Flint's "plain speaking and dealing" was almost guaranteed not to endear the young minister to his parishioners.

An example such as the above might well be explained away on the grounds of that overzealousness which folklore teaches one to expect on the part of the callow. But Flint seems to have positively looked for ways to make himself disagreeable. On one occasion he exchanged pulpits for a Sunday with a neighboring minister, and two of his own parishioners—apparently two of the few friends he had left in the parish—instead of staying at Lunenburg followed him to hear him preach in his borrowed pulpit. This so annoyed Flint that he refused to speak to his loyal if misguided disciples.

At times, Flint's battles with his recalcitrant parish take on a humorous tinge. Flint was never an easy man to get along with once his ire had been aroused and, as I have tried to show, he was always prone to confuse plain speaking with positive rudeness. Once one of his neighbors, perhaps well-meaning, called on him to admonish him about his unfavorable reputation among his parishioners. When the visitor left, Flint walked with him to the gate and pointed to a place beside the fence, accompanying his gesture with the admonition, "When you have another load to dump, leave it there and don't bring it into the house."

In addition to these personal tiffs with the members of his flock, there seems to have been some opinion in the parish at large that the new minister was lax in his duties. When Flint had originally been called to Lunenburg, he had agreed to preach two services each Sunday, one in the morning and one in the afternoon. The work apparently proved too much for him— throughout his life his health was always precarious—and in 1809, at his request, his duties were reduced to one service. Taken by itself this incident proves very little, though Kirkpatrick remarks the ungraciousness in the congregation's accession to their minister's request; but, when coupled with the accusation that Flint was careless in keeping his records, the researcher may well suspect that the congregation, rightly or wrongly, felt that Flint was remiss in his duties. This latter charge, it should be remarked, apparently has some justice to it. Flint seems to have made returns of marriage ceremonies he had performed only about every three years, and then without dates. In a parish the size of Lunenburg the record-keeping can certainly not have been particularly onerous. Indeed, the birth dates of none of the three children born to Flint at Lunenburg— Micah (1803), Emeline Hubbard (1805), and Ebenezer Hubbard (1808)—are recorded; there are only the baptismal dates of the first two.

Whatever the rights and wrongs of the in-fighting between Flint and his parish, it is obvious that the real difficulty was one of personalities. Perhaps Flint's youth aggravated his arrogance and lack of tact; certainly the townspeople soon discovered that they did not really care for their young minister. The final break came, not surprisingly, over an argument about salary. In 1814 Flint asked for a raise. Certainly justice was on his side. His salary had not been changed since he had accepted the call, and even in 1814, $400 was not a princely emolument, especially for a husband with a wife and three children to feed. Yet the real issue here was not a simple one of salary. Apparently Flint had so antagonized the townspeople that they were using this dispute as a lever to force his resignation. They succeeded. Flint resigned, pleading his inability to do further good for the parish and claiming bad health. His resignation was accepted, and on June 14, 1814, he was relieved of his duties as pastor, though he lived on in Lunenburg for another fifteen months. His successor, the Reverend David Damon, was appointed at a salary of $600.

So, at thirty-four years of age, Flint resigned his pastorate and gave up his career in an atmosphere of bitterness and recrimination. The impression we get of him is that of a headstrong man, not so much unwilling to compromise as unable to communicate. Doubtless his youthful ideals had received a severe blow, and probably his disillusion was the greater since his expectations had been unrealistically great. Yet the disappointment, one feels, was more at the fact of having failed than at his inability in a pastoral role. Beginning one's life over at thirty-four is not an easy step, especially for a man untrained in any profession but the one he finds uncongenial, and with wife and three children as hostages to fortune. It is not surprising, therefore, that before breaking entirely with the ministry Flint was to try his hand at missionary work. As a missionary Flint might preach—and numerous witnesses attest that he preached well—without at the same time having the responsibilities of a parish. He might also, he probably thought, be more effective in converting unbelievers than in haggling with parishioners; and, finally, in missionary work he might salvage something from the wreck of the past fourteen years.

Nonetheless, the dismissal rankled. In his most autobiographical novel, *George Mason* (1829), Flint gives us his side of the story. George Mason's father, the Reverend Mason, has emigrated to the West from a small parish much like Lunenburg. His reasons for leaving may well have been Flint's in a similar situation:

Few of my readers would comprehend the peculiar trials of a minister in such a place, or would be able to understand the complication of minute difficulties and vexations, which, during a ministry of sixteen years, in a country village, had broken down his health and spirits, and finally induced him to ask a dismission from his people . . . His parish comprehended every shade of opinion in religion and politics. Embittered parties and eternal disputations were the consequence. In attempting to keep clear of all, the pastor became embroiled with all. . . . The salary was small, and the family increasing. He became poor, and obnoxious both to the religious and political parties; and after sixteen years of the prime of his life spent among them, admitting, the while, that he was exemplary, of good feelings, learned and eloquent, they refused him, in town-meeting, a request to add something to his salary. In disgust he asked a dismission, and it was granted (15).

Fifteen years after the event the wound still hurt. The passage can safely be read as autobiographical. The only change from Flint's own life is the fact that Reverend Mason spent sixteen years as an unappreciated pastor, while Flint had spent only twelve. But Flint was to sever all formal connections with the ministry in 1818 when he resigned from the Missionary Society of Connecticut, sixteen years after his ordination. In *George Mason* he expresses his bitterness not only with his parishioners at Lunenburg but with his entire earlier career.

Yet Flint was not only to remember his parishioners with dislike. In 1825 he returned to Lunenburg for a visit, and justly remarked in his *Recollections* that "all that ought to have been remembered by my former people in my favour, was remembered. All that in those days of inexperience, of untamed youth and temperament, related to me, which I could have wished forgotten, seemed to have been completely consigned to oblivion" (388).

III *Literary Importance of the Lunenburg Years*

Probably the most significant aspect of Flint's career in the ministry is one which would not have occurred to him at the time—its influence on his literary endeavors. For his experiences in Lunenburg and as a missionary left an indelible impression not only on his thought but on his literary style.

It would indeed be surprising if so many years in the ministry had not left some imprint on Flint's thought, especially in view of the fact that his disillusion with the religious life was not with the Christian faith itself but only with some temporal aspects of the church militant. And much of Flint's later writing does show a strong religious bias. Literature for Flint was always ethical in purpose and generally didactic in form. Typically the ostensible reason for his literary work is, he says, to adduce to moral perfection, or to cozen the reader into the practice of virtue. The moral of the story of *George Mason*, for instance, is straightforwardly stated at the beginning of the book: says Flint, "the moral and the maxim which I wish to inculcate is, that we ought never to despond, either in our religious or our temporal trials" (3-4). *Arthur Clenning* (1828) is written, Flint avows, because of its good moral effect (I, 17-18). The "principal object" of *The Lost Child* (1830), Flint advises his "young readers," is "to soften ... their young hearts to pity and all good feelings" and, more specifically, "to impress upon them, that parents, who are really religious and devout, have strong consolations in deep affliction from trust in God" (4). He translates *The Art of Being Happy* (1832) because it inculcates "the truth that *virtue is happiness*" (iii), and he justifies his translation of *The Bachelor Reclaimed* (1834) on the specific grounds that the work "inculcate[s] elevation and purity of mind, and a useful moral," namely "the triumph of love over the most inveterate and rooted prejudices" (v).

It is not too farfetched to see in Flint's didactic purpose a reflection of the views expressed in his *Sermon Preached ... at the Ordination of the Rev. Ebenezer Hubbard* mentioned above. For the purpose of literature, as Flint sees it, is very similar to the role of biblical exempla in the process of conversion. Just as exhortations based on the Gospel adduce to piety, so do the accounts of fictional characters overcoming temptation adduce to virtue.

The Bible, of course, has one advantage in moral persuasion which is denied to fiction; the fact that it is true. For Flint, the truth of a story, if it adduces to moral virtue, is an additional point in its favor. In his own writing Flint constantly remarks the truth of the story he is about to relate. *Francis Berrian* (1826) is addressed to Henry Bullard with the notation that "you well know, that no inconsiderable portion of these adventures is any thing, rather than fiction" (I, iii). *The Lost Child* is not only an inspiring tale, but "the chief facts, related in it, are true" (3), and this point in its favor obviously gives Flint more belief in its efficacy as an agent of moral suasion than if it had been only a fiction, no matter how uplifting.

If part of the ethical value of fiction lies in its approach to truth, it should come as no surprise that the study of objective truth itself leads to ethical revelations. This is very obviously the basis of Flint's lifelong interest in history. For to Flint as to his Puritan ancestors history is the record of God's providence working on earth, of "the slow, but certain and irresistible progress of knowledge and truth."[10] And of course biography—history in its most particular form—combines the general ethical virtue of truth with the hortatory value of specific incident. The *Biographical Memoir of Daniel Boone* (1833) appeals not only to historians who wish to know the facts about the past but to any of those "who have hearts to admire nobility imparted by nature's great seal" ([7]). And the study of the pioneer character as delineated in *Indian Wars of the West* (1833) offers "a new and more elevated standard of imitation to their posterity," for "it can never be useless to contemplate these images of stern self control, of sublime vigor and perseverance." The reason is perfectly clear: for "in seeing what men have been, and may be, we find the best incitements to arrest the downward tendency to indolence, self indulgence, and pusillanimity" (13).

This last example has brought us back again to our first in the *Sermon*. For the lives of the pioneers, like "the simplicity and energy of gospel motives," are not "the idle efforts" of an author's "own talents and invention" but truths direct from the hand of God.

The study of science can also lead to moral virtue, and this explains Flint's interest in it. In his eyes, however, the study of God's works is not important in itself but because it leads man to God. Flint's study of science is, therefore, primarily theological. Paley's famous proof of the existence of God—when one finds a watch, one infers a watchmaker—is the implicit justification for scientific study in Flint's view. In his *Lectures Upon Natural History* (1833) he points out that Galen was reclaimed from atheism by examining the human body—Galen apparently needed more than a watch—and, if we need more than Galen, we will find the universe an even more convincing proof of the existence of God than the body. "Where the term *nature* is used," he says, "I would be understood to mean *Providence* or *God*." In this example Flint goes farther than Paley; for Paley would admit that, though a watch implies a watchmaker, yet the study of the watch does not necessarily lead to him. The watch can be legitimately studied in and for itself. Flint, on the other hand, more or less equates the study of science with that of God. Science and religion not only do not conflict; science is almost a branch of theology: "In the heavens and the earth, in man that thinks, and the insect that creeps, I have found every thing labelled with the single, grand, all comprehending term—God" (vii-viii).

It is not particularly remarkable that a former minister should keep some trace of his religious convictions in his later thought. But it is worthy of more than passing notice that Flint's experience in the ministry seems to have influenced not only his philosophical views but also his literary style. Flint's later rhetorical style is strongly influenced by that of the pulpit, and it has probably already occurred to the reader of this essay that his method of literary presentation often strongly resembles that of the polemical sermon. Indeed, in form Flint's novels and stories often resemble sermons. They begin with an overt statement of a moral proposition which they then prove. The story is subsumed to the text which precedes it, and is in fact a moral exemplum of the proposition stated. The philosophical notion is explicitly given; the fiction is adduced to prove it.

In the *Sermon* to which I have so often referred is an interesting passage which may well throw considerable light on Flint's literary method. Just previous to it Flint has been considering the results of conversion, and he proceeds to show us the joy of the regenerate sinner by means of a fictional example:

> *A soul is saved from death;* and, as one of the last blessed results of his conversion, let us behold the renovated sinner, returning to the bosom of his own family. How touching and solemn the scene! He had been a prodigal in a strange land, herding with the vilest of the vile. He had grieved all that concerned themselves to think of him. He had wounded his connexions in the tenderest part. Perhaps worse; depending on him, and connected with him, the innocent suffered not only poverty, but shame and reproach with the guilty. Behold him regardless of their wants, ferocious and cruel; his sensibilities benumbed; his heart hardened, and incapable of the domestic sympathies, which cannot, at least, in any considerable degree, inhere in a

heart, which has not been softened by religion. Behold him not only denying the sustaining hand, to lead them over the rough and rugged ways of life, but doubling their burdens with ferocity, and enervating their courage by superadding to their load, *a wounded spirit*, incapable of bearing up against the ills of life.

Consider this man, at length reclaimed from *the error of his way*. The adamant of his heart, as the rock smitten by Moses, flows with penitential sorrow. He raises his eyes once more to the heavens. "I have sinned, father, against heaven, and in thy sight." Behold him returning to that mansion, so dreary and joyless. His ferocity has become mildness. The tiger is changed to a lamb. The barbarian has felt the spirit of Christ, and, struck with horror at what he lately was, becomes doubly assiduous to discharge all the affectionate offices of domestic life. Who cannot fancy the scene? what kind greetings! what congratulations! How pleasant to behold *kindred and friends dwelling together in unity*. It is as the *dew of Hermon descending upon the mountains of the Lord*. He is now affectionate and kind in all the domestic relations; a good parent, a good citizen, a man contented and happy, rejoicing in the *peace passing all understanding*, the *joy unspeakable and full of glory*, resulting from the consciousness that he is in the same road with all, who are travelling up to the holy hill, and that he shall increase the number of the blessed (11-12).

First of all, we should notice the quality of the rhetoric of this sermon. As is not particularly surprising, the rhetorical style is closer to spoken than to written English usage. What is noteworthy, however, is the fact that this same spoken oratorical rhetoric becomes the basic style of Flint's later writing. At times this can cause some confusion. Note, for example, the sentence near the beginning of the quotation: "Behold him regardless of their wants, ferocious and cruel." In spoken English the meaning of this sentence is perfectly clear; but technically the syntax makes the wants ferocious and cruel, rather than the sinner. Many critics have pointed out Flint's hastiness in revision and his apparent gaucheries of style. On examination, however, the gaucheries will generally be found not to be blunders alone but rather the looser idiom of spoken English applied in a situation where the more formal written idiom is required.

The nearness of Flint's written style to that of spoken English is emblematic of something more basic to his literary method than a mere trick of rhetoric. For Flint seems to think of the author as someone who is, in the narrowest sense of the word, *telling* a story. His rhetorical method has the effect of always intruding the author into the reader's consciousness. Often Flint is not content only to insist on his authorial presence through the force of his style alone. A feature of his later literary method will be the way in which he directly addresses the reader, just as in this sermon he rhetorically includes the audience with him in the consideration of the exemplum he is about to elucidate. "Consider this man, at length reclaimed from *the error of his way*," says Flint in the beginning of the second paragraph of the quotation, before plunging into the consideration itself. A similar device is commonplace in his fictional style. "Bitterly were these parents punished for this injudicious and unjust fondness [for *The Lost Child*]" (16), he tells us before going on to show what the punishment entailed. He often attempts to engage our attention in one of his stories by avowing his own personal interest in it, a device similar in both intention and performance to the more simple authorial comment discussed above. And often he will intrude some kind of personal authorial relation into a work where it is totally unnecessary.

The best example of this last is in the *Lectures Upon Natural History* (1833), where the entire format of the book is unnecessary to the subject matter. For the *Lectures* are not lectures at all, but merely divisions of subject matter into chapters. By treating the material as though it were a series of lectures, Flint is able, however, to assume the oratorical position toward his material of a lecturer addressing an audience, a position which he makes explicit in the Preface to the *Lectures,* where he particularly recommends them to students. Similarly, the *Recollections of the Last Ten Years* is ostensibly a collection of letters from Timothy Flint to his cousin James. Actually, the division of the work into letters is highly arbitrary, but the device serves the purpose of allowing the author to intrude his own personal observations into the book under the guise of private comments to his cousin. Both *Arthur Clenning* and *Francis Berrian* claim to be direct reporting; the first is allegedly nothing other than a journal kept by Arthur Clenning, and the latter purports to be the record of a long monologue on the part of Berrian, whom Flint has met by chance on a Mississippi steamboat. The device in *Arthur Clenning* is exactly the same as that in the *Recollections*. Through the medium of the journal Flint may introduce comments on the action and authorial reflections which supposedly were made by Clenning himself. In *Francis Berrian* the author and his hero are often indistinguishable, and Berrian's reflections on the significance of his own adventures are often clearly Flint's own half-concealed admonitions to the audience to pay attention.

The purpose of this device is—as may most clearly be seen in the *Lectures Upon Natural History*—to make the subject matter of a work more interesting by involving the reader in the personality of its author. The danger, particularly in a work of fiction, lies in the fact that the work may never become anything other than an extension of its author's personal remarks.

Another interesting feature of Flint's style which may be noticed in the *Sermon* is its peculiar limitation of range. Though the prose is emphatic, it is at the same time peculiarly uncompelling. It is the hyperbolic prose of overstatement; and, without the relief of ordinary prose, it soon becomes tedious. Flint never really learns how to use understatement for esthetic effect. His style lacks any change of pace, and soon cloys because of its sameness. If the reader takes the trouble to read aloud the long exemplum from the *Sermon* quoted above, it is possible to speak it quite effectively. But it is possible only by varying the rhetoric by means of vocal emphasis and—assuming one were in the pulpit—gesture. In short, this hyperbolic rhetoric becomes effective only when one is able in some way to get behind it, when one has in fact the author before one to read the passage aloud. This is all very well in a sermon, but it does not work so successfully in a book, where the rhetoric must stand by itself without any outside interpretation. Flint never really understands this. The greatest weakness of his prose style is always a tendency to write as if he were speaking; as a result his prose, no matter how vehement, is often flat and sometimes dull.

Finally, if we look generally rather than particularly at the *Sermon,* another peculiarity of Flint's style emerges. This is the strikingly abstract quality of its rhetoric. In this exemplum what Flint does is to give us a plot summary which, in the hands of another author, could be indefinitely expanded. We have a "renovated sinner" presented to us: First his past life is summarized—he has been a "prodigal in a strange land," careless of the wants of those dependent upon him; then the results of his conversion are placed before our eyes—his reception by his family is mentioned and his later life is summarized. We leave him "a good parent, a good citizen, a man contented and happy." We have, in other words, a summary of his entire life.

Yet this summary is strange in that it is not really that of the life of a particular sinner so much as it is a didactic statement of the nature of sin-in-general coupled with a theoretical statement about the nature of redemption. The personal characteristics of the particular sinner are unimportant. The hero of Flint's exemplum is no particular character to whose life he draws our attention in order that we may find some moral truth prefigured in it. Flint works from a general example in order to draw a general conclusion, rather than using a particular instance to achieve the same result. This method of handling his fictional material is basic to his later writing.

We should note at this point that this method of presenting fictional material by means of general statement is by no means an inevitable result of an early training in the theory and practice of writing sermons. Many sermons work on precisely the opposite principle from Flint's—a principle which is closer to twentieth-century esthetic theory. This is the notion that particular examples are more effective than general statements, if only because we find it difficult to involve ourselves emotionally with too broad a philosophic generalization. Chaucer's Pardoner, for example, himself no mean rhetorician, when preaching on the text *Radix malorum est cupiditas,* invites us to consider the case of "Thise riotoures thre of which I telle," who "Longe erst er prime rong of any belle, / Were set hem in a taverne for to drynke," and, once having defined his three characters and placed them specifically in a particular tavern, he proceeds to tell a unique history of greed and its results. To take a more nearly contemporary example, Melville's Father Mapple, preaching on the biblical "yarn" of Jonah and the Whale, actually interpolates particular incidents into the story to make its meaning clearer. To take a clear example, he expands Jonah 1:3, "But Jonah rose up to flee unto Tarshish from the presence of the Lord, and went down to Joppa; and he found a ship going to Tarshish; so he paid the fare thereof and went down into it, to go with them unto Tarshish from the presence of the Lord," into a chatty paragraph of several hundred words, including personal descriptions of Jonah, and completely unauthorized remarks about his appearance on the part of the crew—"Jack, he's robbed a widow," "Joe, do you mark him; he's a bigamist," and "Harry lad, I guess he's the adulterer that broke jail in old Gomorrah, or belike, one of the missing murderers from Sodom."

These two very different examples have one important thing in common: both attempt to engage the hearer's interest by involving him personally in the scene. Flint, on the contrary, strives to gain his emotional effect by appealing to the reader to supply, out of his own experience, the emotional context to the story he is narrating; in short, he removes the reader from direct participation in the narrative. "How pleasant to behold kindred and friends dwelling together in unity," says Flint; but the details of this pleasant scene are left to our imaginations.

This reliance on the general statement, to the bare bones of which the reader relates his own experience in order to achieve any kind of emotional response, is central to Flint's artistic method. It explains the almost total lack of dialogue in his work, though dialogue is often given to us in paraphrase, sometimes with the adjuration that we supply, from our own knowledge of the human heart, the exact wording. It explains as well Flint's method of telling a tale. Flint, for reasons I have suggested above, conceives a fictional situation as a depiction of a life history. But he generally does not tell his history by dwelling on a few important scenes in the life of his hero which are in some way central to his development. Rather he tends to give a chronology of his hero's life and, to twentieth-century taste at least, to underemphasize the importance of particular events. In *George Mason,* for instance, he relieves himself of the responsibility for enlarging on the circumstances of the death of Mr. Mason by remarking that "if the bare recounting them does not make my reader feel the situation of Mr. Mason, I am aware, that nothing, which I can say, will do it" (37-38). In other words, the reader must, from his own knowledge of human nature, supply the emotional context to the scene. More significant, perhaps, in the same novel, is his explanation for not detailing at greater length the personal histories of the main characters. "I find myself entering too minutely into the fortunes of this family," he says, "and I must hasten to follow the thread of events by a more general outline" (113).

By this approach Flint obviously hopes to gain a certain universality of appeal. Everyone, his argument seems to be, has in his mind's eye a more perfect picture of a given event than can be introduced by the most cunning pen. As a result, an esthetic literary effect can best be produced by indicating to the reader what picture should be conjured up, and then letting him supply the details for himself. At its worst, this method is reminiscent of the old saw about the jokester's convention where, to save time, witticisms were told by number; when someone said "Twenty-four," everyone else laughed. At its best, however, the method serves to give a rather striking universal quality to Flint's fictional pictures.

Two examples may make the point clearer. At one place in *Francis Berrian* a young Englishman is badly injured in a mining accident, and Berrian goes to visit him. He reflects that the Englishman "appeared in an agony of pain, and the noble effort which he made to suppress the expression of it before his mother, gave his countenance a striking moral interest" (I, 179-80). Even without benefit of Hemingway, we feel disappointed by this. The picture Flint expects us to conjure up is, if anything, ludicrous, and whatever "striking moral interest" may inhere in the Englishman's grimaces must be explicated in order to make us aware of it. The scene cries for dialogue, or at the very least for more minute description.

On the other hand consider this description of a horse race, from *George Mason*.

> Long before the race was started, there had been a number of fist-fights, in which the eyes of the parties about to bet, were bunged up, that their judgments might be less diverted by visible objects from a sagacious calculation in regard to the issue of the race. Here might be seen, in a concentrated form, the readiness of the American people, to form parties, and to be stirred up by the fury of party spirit. A bully comes forward, and

cries out, "The Green Mantle beats the field," adding an oath, that I choose to omit. "Here's my fist for five dollars, and a fight for Green Mantle." "Done," says another; "ten to your five, and here's at you." Upon the word, they fall to it, and fight, until one, or the other, is *hors du combat* (109).

Here the method is much more successful. Though the picture is still general, we have no difficulty supplying the details from our mind's eye. The speakers are not individualized, but their speech is sharply defined, and though the ostensible moral to the story—"the readiness of the American people, to form parties"—does in fact have a sort of crazy relevance to what is actually going on, it does not limit the scene to a sterile didacticism.

IV *Emigration to the West*

Whatever ultimate influence the Lunenburg pastorate may have had on Flint's future literary career, in 1814 a career as a man of letters was twelve years in the future, and Flint had not apparently anticipated any such move. Logically enough, he sought some other method of support within the only profession for which he had been trained—the ministry; and, not surprisingly, he saw the opportunities furnished by the missionary societies.

The early nineteenth-century missionary society came into prominence as a response to changing conditions in American social history. As Americans emigrated westward, they left behind them the ecclesiastical organization of their fathers. In fact they left all ecclesiastical organization behind, and it was widely feared that they might leave behind all religious belief as well. To cope with this horrendous possibility was the purpose of the various missionary societies, whose intention was not primarily to convert the heathen but to reclaim the lapsed. In order to accomplish this intent, the various societies sent missionaries to preach in areas where there was no formal ecclesiastical organization. The purpose of this missionary activity was not only to preach but to form churches. Typically, if all went well, the missionary would succeed in awakening enough religious feeling in the emerging backwoods community so that some of its citizens would take the initiative in forming a

regular church. Missionaries were customarily paid a flat salary
and liberally supplied with tracts and religious literature. As
a rule they also took up a collection when they preached, but
whatever money was taken in was customarily returned to the
missionary society and was used for expenses and, hopefully,
to send other missionaries into the field. The advantage of the
system was that ministers could at least occasionally visit areas
whose population was either too sparse, too poor, or too indifferent to support a regular church. The primary difference
between these societies and modern missionary movements is
that they were conceived of not as a more or less permanent
agency to the heathen but as a temporary group whose purpose
was ultimately to bring a more stable ecclesiastical organization
to the frontier.

Flint's first experience as a missionary was under the auspices
of the Massachusetts Society for Promoting Christian Knowledge.
In the summer and autumn of 1814 he was sent to New Hampshire. Later he was sent on another mission, probably to western
Massachusetts and to New York. But he did not remain long
with the society; he resigned apparently because of what he
considered its intolerance and narrow-mindedness.

In 1815 Flint made up his mind to emigrate to the West, and
he received a commission from the Missionary Society of Connecticut to preach in such settlements of the states of Ohio
and Kentucky as he should think proper. Later his territory
was extended to include Missouri as well. His reasons for making
the decision to leave New England can only be conjectured. In
a letter of July 23, 1815, he pleads ill health as a major factor
in his decision, and mentions the hope that the milder climate
of the West may prove beneficial. But, since this letter was
written to the society before Flint's actual appointment was
certain, it is difficult to tell just how much reliance should be
placed upon it. Flint also mentions, in this letter, the fact that
in the West he hopes "to establish in some central place a
religious publication, like our religious monthly papers; except
that it should more particularly vindicate our literature, charities
and institutions." This is the first mention, on his part, of any
specific literary ambitions. Not until twelve years later, in 1827,
was he actually to establish such a publication, the *Western*

Monthly Review; and, when he did, it was completely independent of formal religious sponsorship.

An important consideration in his decision to emigrate must also have been economic. The appointment was one of considerable importance, and Flint must have hoped the salary would be commensurate. On paper it was. He was given $25.00 a week by the society, more than three times as much as he had received from the parish of Lunenburg. Yet the hoped-for economic gain apparently proved illusory. Flint had failed to reckon with his increased expenses, which had to be defrayed from his salary; he also assumed that the cost of living was lower in the West than in New England, an assumption which proved false. In 1816 he petitioned the society for an increase in salary, pleading that his present wages covered only one-half of his expenses. He also asked for permission to keep whatever collections he made, and this request was apparently granted. He was, however, still quite poor, as the collections were not large. For a three-week missionary tour of Kentucky he received a mere $51.50 in collections, and for four months in the Ohio Valley he reported only $66.25 in receipts.

To get from Lunenburg to Cincinnati, Flint and his family traveled overland with all their worldly goods in a two-horse wagon. At Pittsburgh they sold the wagon and went on in a flatboat skippered by an incompetent seaman who almost upset them. As a result of this experience they bought their own boat and undertook to transport themselves downstream. But Flint's health was not equal to the strain of handling a large open boat, and he and the rest of his family became so ill that they were forced to lay over in Wheeling. The whole family then took passage in a keelboat to Marietta, where they had friends. After recovering there, they bought a flatboat and set off down the river again, arriving at Cincinnati without further disaster, where they settled for the winter.

The experiences of this voyage were chronicled much later in the *Recollections of the Last Ten Years* which was, however, based on letters written during or shortly after the journey. In the *Recollections* we get a fascinating picture of Flint's gradual change in attitude toward the West. We see him at first at a loss in this strange environment, and one of the dominant notes of the *Recollections* is that of homesickness. But as the book progresses the homesickness becomes less real and more conventional, and the memory of New England fades before the charm and vigor of the West. Flint's report of his journey is in many ways almost a classic study of the theme of the dude who goes West. It begins by deploring the Westerners' lack of New England—and hence civilized—standards, and it ends with the author's almost complete conversion to the Westerners' point of view. Even in Cincinnati in 1816 Flint is beginning to discover in himself a reluctant admiration for Westerners, despite their rough-and-ready ways. Their life, he sees, is hard, and this condition explains their lack of polish.

At times on his trip Flint is very much the man of God, shocked and appalled by the crudity of the natives. The teamsters who drive between Philadelphia and Pittsburgh are, he says in the *Recollections,* "more rude, profane, and selfish, than either sailors, boatmen, or hunters." Determined to do something about the profanity at least, and perhaps with one eye cocked on the Missionary Society's approval, he goes on to tell how "I often dropped among them, as by accident, that impressive tract, the 'Swearer's Prayer.' I was pleased to remark the result of their reflections, as they read the tract, apart on their window-seats. In some it seemed to produce a momentary thoughtfulness; in others a smile; and again in others, a deep growl of acquiescence, very like that which every one has heard, who has attended a council of Indians, and heard them express a kind of reluctant assent to terms proposed to them" (8-9).

Swearing was always Flint's particular abhorrence, but before very long on his journey he had come to understand how to combat this particular manifestation of the powers of blackness more effectively than by means of the "Swearer's Prayer." The first step of course involved the rather sophisticated realization that blasphemy in the West was not exactly comparable to blasphemy in New England. Though Flint never admits that profanity is an absolute necessity in either region, he very soon picks up the rather profound insight that, whatever its religious consequences, blasphemy is not always intended in this world as a personal insult. While traveling down the Ohio, he notes an example of the Western folk-humor of conversation by means of choice abusive epithets. Flint discovers that, when boats on the Ohio pass people on shore the boatmen hail the landsmen in rather straightforward terms, a practice known as "blackguarding." Flint disapproves; but he still sees the humor. "I have more than once been compelled to smile, at the readiness or whimsicality of the retorts in these trials of vulgarity, between the people on shore and the boatmen," he says (31).

On the last leg of the trip Flint met his first frontiersman, "a fine, healthy-looking Kentuckian" with his wife, children, and a few Negroes, all going West. He told the man of his abhorrence of swearing, and the Kentuckian, civilly enough, agreed not to swear since it bothered others of the company. Flint obviously approved of this chance acquaintance, possibly because of some fancied resemblance in their situations. For Kentucky had grown too small for him, just as New England had for Flint: "Land had already become too scarce and dear. He wanted elbow-room, did not wish to have a neighbour within three miles of him, and was moving to the upper Mississippi, for range" (34). The two men seem to have hit it off very well, a real compliment to Flint's adaptability. But more important, Flint, in a few short weeks had learned a valuable lesson in getting along with people. He had gained his objective of stopping the man's swearing without losing his friendship. What would the Kentuckian have thought if some "pilgrim" had presented him with a copy of the "Swearer's Prayer"!

It is not necessary to detail all the events of Flint's later life in the West. Until 1818 he remained a missionary. During this time he lived in Cincinnati, and then in St. Louis and St. Charles, Missouri. In his missionary work he traveled through Ohio, Indiana, Kentucky, and Missouri, often on horseback or by primitive river boat. On occasion even these methods of transportation failed and he had to walk from backwoods settlement to backwoods settlement. The hardness of this life wrought a deterioration in his never too robust constitution, and in August and September of 1818, just after resigning from the society, he was seriously ill with the "seasoning fever," and for a time his life was despaired of.

His final resignation from the ministry, like his first resignation at Lunenburg, seems to have been caused primarily by his outspokenness; though this time he offended not only his congregations but also the officialdom of the society. The society had sent the Reverend Salmon Giddings to Missouri as well as

Flint, and the two men did not get along well. In 1817 Giddings felt it necessary to report to the society that Flint was universally disliked by the people of St. Charles, who considered him, Giddings said, "a Speculator, Avaricious, Immoral and of course not a Christian." The first two charges refer to Flint's desperate attempts to supplement his meager income by various expedients, among them a school and an unfortunate investment in a store in St. Louis. Public opinion was outraged by a man of God who engaged in such worldly pursuits—without, however, taking any concrete steps to remove the necessity for him to do so. One year Flint did not receive enough money from contributions to pay the cost of his ferriage across the river.

The charges of immorality and non-Christian belief, though without any factual basis, again show Flint's almost uncanny ability to alienate congregations. Apparently he was rather too outspoken in his preaching for the public taste, attacking, among other things, public non-observance of the Sabbath. Although Sunday balls were the fashion in St. Charles, one time Flint reported these frivolous violators of the law to the grand jury—dancing on the Sabbath being illegal—and they were subsequently punished. Like his earlier resort to law in Lunenburg, Flint's victory in St. Charles was a Pyrrhic one. People merely stopped coming to hear him preach.

Flint also seems to have made enemies within the bureaucracy of the society, as charges of incompetence were brought against him. If by incompetence is meant the incontrovertible fact that Flint had absolutely no personal gift for missionary work, the charge is doubtless true. But Flint, always honest to a fault, was guilty as well of the more serious crime of not sending back those glowing reports of ministerial progress in which the society sought aid and comfort. In 1817 he reported that, despite all missionary work, Missouri was still as heathen as Hindustan; and he had suggested earlier that reports of missionary progress had been highly colored in order to please the Eastern members of the society. He remarked that his congregations were not growing—hardly surprising in view of the circumstances—and suggested it was useless to found churches in such barren soil. Finally, in August, 1817, he wrote the society that he was of so little use that he would soon have to stop taking their money. When, on June 3, 1818, he heard of the charges brought against him by Mr. Giddings, he resigned, one suspects with relief.

Before resigning from the society, Flint had been looking elsewhere for means of support. He had thought of teaching school and preaching, and had had a few invitations. He accepted one from Washington, near Natchez, Mississippi, and, in April, 1819, started south with his family. They got as far as the Arkansas River where they decided to stay for the summer before continuing south, but the entire family became sick, and Flint, fearing for the health of all, decided to retreat to St. Charles. The family started back up the river in October, driving their boat by hand against the current. All of them were weakened by illness, and some days the boys were so sick with the ague that Flint worked alone, dragging the six-ton boat upstream. He estimated later in the *Recollections* that they were able to travel an average of only about twelve miles a day against the current of the Mississippi. Winter was closing in, and they feared that they might have to lay over somewhere along shore for the winter. Provisions also were running low and, when a boat loaded with flour and pork passed them, the boatmen took advantage of their distress by overcharging them for supplies. On November 26 they tied up along shore to shelter from an approaching storm, and there Mrs. Flint gave birth to an infant daughter who lived only two and one half days, and was buried on a high bank beside the "wicked river." The rest of the family doggedly pushed on upstream, arriving by the middle of December at New Madrid, Missouri, where they spent the winter.

In the spring of 1820 they continued their slow progress northward to Jackson, Missouri, where their fifth child—the fourth to live—James Timothy, was born on June 8, 1821. By mid-October, 1821, they were back in St. Charles, two and one half years after so hopefully leaving it. Scarcely had they settled there when all were again taken ill with the ague. Flint, one feels out of desperation, had obtained the lease of a farm four miles from St. Charles, and determined to farm it for subsistence. But by the beginning of 1822, destitute and in poor health, the family decided to renounce the high hopes with which they had approached the West and to return to New England.

The disastrous trip south and the return to Missouri of the

years 1819-22 represents the low point of the family fortunes, and their determination to return to New England, though never carried out, was a tacit admission that they had been beaten by circumstance. Though they had decided to return home, they were unable to put their plan into operation since they were completely destitute. Flint swallowed his pride enough to write the Missionary Society of Connecticut and petition for financial aid, but apparently none was forthcoming. In the summer of 1822 all the family had between them and starvation was the farm on which they had succeeded in building a rude log cabin, the charity of kind neighbors, and whatever small donations Flint received for itinerant preaching. Since no funds could be laid by to defray the expense of the overland journey to New England, they again committed themselves in the autumn of 1822 to the river in a flatboat for the longer but less expensive water journey home by way of the Mississippi to New Orleans and then by sailing vessel to New England.

On this trip south Flint's bad fortune began to change. After visiting New Orleans and Florida he settled, in 1823, in Alexandria, Louisiana, a place to which he had had a call in the dark days of 1817 when his missionary career was turning out so badly. At Alexandria was a small college over which Flint presided, and his duties included preaching as well. For the first time since 1802 the family had enough money to live in modest comfort; more important, the inhabitants of Alexandria were courteous and friendly to Flint and his family. Not only were they sympathetic to his ministerial efforts, but they were personally hospitable, and the family made many warm personal friends.

The most important of these friends was Judge Henry Bullard, whom Flint met in Alexandria and whose personal experiences form most of the background material of Flint's first novel, *Francis Berrian*. The two men were completely congenial: though Bullard was eight years younger than Flint, they were both Harvard graduates, and they were both cultivated men of literary and historical tastes. Indeed, in later life both were elected members of the Massachusetts Historical Society.

All was, however, not perfect. Flint's health, never strong, deteriorated rapidly; and even Judge Bullard's heroic cure, a long horseback trip to the *terra incognita* beyond Natchitoches, did not aid his recovery. In April, 1825, too weak to sit a horse, Flint sailed for New England; he was so ill that, when he arrived at Salem, he said he "had come home to die." His cousin James nursed him back to health, and by September, 1825, Flint had returned to Alexandria. James had encouraged Flint's latent literary ambitions, and while he was convalescing he roughed out his first book, the *Recollections of the Last Ten Years.* James Flint's influence and encouragement were apparently just what Flint needed to determine him finally on a literary career. On the return trip to Alexandria he began work on *Francis Berrian,* and from this time until failing health forced cancellation of all his activities he devoted himself almost exclusively to literary composition.

It is of more than casual significance that after his recovery, Flint returned to Alexandria. Some time between the disastrous years of 1817-22 and 1825 he had finally cast his lot with the West. After the *Recollections,* which are largely the record of Flint's early desperate struggle against poverty, ill health and discouragement, the note of homesickness for New England leaves Flint's writing. He casts his fortune with Alexandria and Cincinnati; and he sees himself no longer as an exile in a strange land but as a quasi-official spokesman for the West and a believer in its ultimate destiny. After the trip home in 1825 to die he never seriously contemplates returning to New England to live, though he does visit it again on occasion and indeed does finally return there to die in 1840.

The exterior circumstances of Flint's life from 1825 on were determined primarily by his failing health. Because of his belief that the hot climate of Alexandria was unhealthy he returned—this time by steamboat—to Cincinnati, where he lived from 1827 to 1833, and where he edited (1827-30) the *Western Monthly Review.* His last child, Martha Elizabeth, was born in Cincinnati in 1828. In 1834, however, he and his family returned to Alexandria, though he himself spent much of his time in travel. His health rapidly deteriorated; from 1834 to 1840 he did little writing. While on a journey to New England he died, on August 16, 1840. His last days had been spent at the home of his brother in North Reading, near where he had been born sixty years before. Four days later he was buried in Salem, where he had spent much of his boyhood and where his family had settled, two hundred years earlier. His cousin James wrote his epitaph:

> He painted on his glowing page,
>   The peerless valley of the West;
> That shall in every coming age,
>   His genius and his toil attest.
>
> But wouldst thou, gentle pilgrim, know
>   What worth, what love, endeared the man?
> This the lone hearts that miss him, show
>   Better than storied marble can.

CHAPTER 2

The Peerless Valley

JAMES FLINT'S epitaph for his cousin Timothy quite accurately reflects contemporary opinion. Though *Francis Berrian*—a novel which has not worn very well—was often mentioned favorably by critics, general opinion of Flint's work was pretty close to his own appraisal of himself: he "did not think he would be remembered as a litterateur, [but] thought he was preserving matters of interest for the future historian."[1] N. P. Willis remarks in particular reference to the *Western Monthly Review* that Flint is "industrious in collecting whatever is important in the antiquities and natural history of the 'Valley of the Mississippi'" and, in another context, that he "is really a man of talent," following this general praise by the specific reminder that "a book of his on the Valley of the Mississippi is very much esteemed in the United States."[2] Flint is one of the very few Americans of whom Mrs. Trollope has anything good to say; but, just as she was perhaps too bitter in her remarks about America in general, so was she rather too sweet in her comments on Flint in particular. Though she mentions his other works favorably, she singles out the *History and Geography of the Mississippi Valley* for particular praise as "a work of great interest and information."[3]

Flint's own high opinion of collectors of information and his related low opinion of imaginative writers may be clearly seen in some of his comments on American literature. An early listing in the *Western Monthly Review* of "Writers of the Western Country" of general rather than local reputation confines itself mostly to scientists, historians, and politicians. A later listing for *The Athenaeum* dwells on American oratory, sermons, medical writers, lawyers, mathematicians, scientists of all types, and American literary reviews; it touches literature scarcely at all.[4] Flint's view of literature, in short, does not confine itself to belles-lettres, and indeed to present taste appears to slight it.

If we wish, we may make a rather arbitrary selection of those works of Flint's which are primarily factual accounts of life in the Mississippi Valley rather than romances based upon it. These would be the *Recollections of the Last Ten Years* (1826), *A Condensed Geography and History of the Western States* (1828) expanded into *The History and Geography of the Mississippi Valley* (1832), and the *Western Monthly Review* (1827-30). In addition, more specific historic information is contained in *Indian Wars of the West* (1833) and in the *Biographical Memoir of Daniel Boone* (1833), which we will consider in the next chapter. These works are all, however, more or less repetitious. Flint quite often uses in later works material which he has previously printed, often with very little or no change between one printing and the next; and he interpolates sections from earlier works into later ones without much revision. Consequently, the best method for elucidating Flint's ideas and opinions about the Mississippi Valley is not by means of a detailed summary of each of these works, but rather by a shorter indication of the contents of each, followed by some general remarks about the tendencies of Flint's views taken as a whole.

I Recollections of the Last Ten Years

The *Recollections of the Last Ten Years* purports—as we have already noted—to be a series of letters from Timothy Flint to his cousin James. There are twenty-seven numbered letters plus another unnumbered one which serves as an epilogue to the book. The letters are not unities in themselves, but serve instead the function of breaking the book into chapters and of giving some order to its rather miscellaneous contents. They are, however, based on real letters which Flint had in front of him as he wrote the book. The use of this real material has one great literary advantage: it gives an air of reality to those scenes in the book which are temporally remote. For example, the first eight letters, describing the Flints' emigration from Lunenburg to Cincinnati in 1815, ten years before the book was written, are as particular in detail and clear in visualization of scene as is the last un-numbered letter, which was written ten years later in 1825. Though Flint always had a good eye for detail, and had a good memory as well, the fact that he had his original letters to refer to when writing nevertheless gives the *Recollections* a vivid quality which they would not otherwise have had.

The format of the *Recollections* is roughly autobiographical. The book begins by detailing the emigration west of Flint and his family, follows them from Cincinnati to Missouri, then down the Mississippi to New Orleans and Alexandria. Into the autobiographical narrative are interpolated general descriptions of the places Flint visits, their history, climate, population, and so on. These interpolated passages are carefully researched and even today are well worth reading for their factual picture of a bygone era. Flint, always a careful and scholarly tourist, was more interested in factual data than in picturesque anecdote, a qualification he himself touches on in the first letter, where he tells his cousin James that he has been over the ground of which he writes and hence—unlike most travelers—is qualified to discuss it with authority. In the *Recollections* he has a rather too conceited view of the value of originality, mentioning (2) that he "can assert, with perfect confidence," that he had "not consulted a book on [the] subject, from the commencement to the close" of the time he was writing the *Recollections*. This know-nothing posture is a feature of only the *Recollections*; in his later works he freely avows his indebtedness to other authors, always claiming, however, that he has modified their work wherever necessary on the basis of his own firsthand knowledge of the region. Even in the *Recollections* this know-nothing posture is more a conventional attitude than a factual statement. His capsule histories of various western communities, for instance, have been carefully worked up from other histori-cal sources.

When the *Recollections* is compared with Flint's later histori-cal writing, one feature stands out prominently: the personal tone of this work as contrasted with the pose of objectivity of Flint's later historical studies. To this reader's taste, the personal "I was there" quality of the *Recollections* is one of the book's most compelling features, and its disappearance from Flint's later historical writing is an unqualified loss. The guise of the personally involved reporter who tells of events which he has witnessed or with which he has been concerned serves not only to give the book a certain interest through detailing the narrator's fortunes but, more important, involves us closely in Flint's world of 1815-25. In a book of—for lack of a better term—social history, the most difficult artistic problem is to capture the mood of the bygone world being described. In the *Recollections*, Flint succeeds admirably; in the later books, no amount of objectivity can recapture the sense of personal involvement of the *Recollections*.

One reason for this is that Flint's method of narration in the *Recollections* requires him to tell almost everything in the first person or, when he does talk in the third person, to imply his own personal presence very close behind the action. Note for example his description of the Indians who had come to St. Louis to make a treaty with the government:

> They were generally dirty, rude, and disposed to intoxication. When ladies of respectable dress and appearance came to see them, as often happened, for they were encamped just out of the limits of the town, they were particular in the manifestation of marks of savage rudeness and indecency. They were well aware of the effect of such conduct, and when the ladies fled in confusion, they were sure to raise a brutal laugh (142-43).

This is a brilliant piece of reporting, even granting the fact that Flint has no sympathy at all with the Indians' point of view. Indians are meant to be looked at and reported on, and perhaps commiserated over, and they had better realize it; Flint has no notion that the Indians might resent being treated as though they were one of the sights to be "seen," and his own moral bias, to put it mildly, is obvious. But the interesting feature of this passage lies in Flint's manner of exemplifying his philosophical point. The story begins with a theoretical statement, in a manner—as I have indicated in the first chapter—typical of Flint's rhetoric: Indians are rude. But to prove this statement, Flint takes us to an actual Indian encampment to show us an incident from real life. How much better this is than the style of Flint's later historical writing may be seen by comparing the above passage with one written later in the *History and Geog-*

raphy of the Mississippi Valley. Here Flint is describing the extinction of the Indians as a race:

> From the apparent incompatibility of the Indian character with the modes and requirements of civilized life, this ill-fated race is every where wasting away, when brought in contact with people of municipal and industrious habits. . . . The most humane exertions have constantly been in operation, on the part of the General Government, to preserve the race from extinction, by severe provisions to prevent their obtaining ardent spirits, and by unwearied efforts to train them to the arts and agriculture, and to impart to them the blessings of education and Christianity (II, 11).

In terms of overall rhetorical structure this passage is much the same as the first one; it begins with a general statement and goes on to prove it. The proof, however, is all by means of general assertive statement, and the impression the passage gives us is one of philosophy at second hand. However true it may be, it is uncompelling.

Though the *Recollections* is our most important biographical source for Flint's life from 1815-25, it is nonetheless certain that Flint's reason for publishing his work is not primarily that of getting his autobiography on record. His purpose in writing was, as ours in reading must be, primarily to give a picture of the nascent Western territories. Yet the personal biographical form of narration serves one other important literary function in the *Recollections* through the exemplification of theme. For the real philosophical "subject" of the *Recollections,* as of all Flint's historical writing, is the triumph of progress; and, as a means to develop this theme of the victory of civilization over barbarism, the method of narration on the basis of personal experience is unexcelled. It will be recalled that Flint's life during the decade which furnished the materials for the *Recollections* was spent in more or less constant travel throughout the Mississippi Valley; and his final literary report of the development of the Western territories dwells on the incredible changes in the face of the country which he personally observed during his ten years on the scene. Flint develops this theme with considerable skill. He constantly draws our attention to the rough-and-ready quality of pioneer life, and contrasts it with the relative comfort of life in the later period. His first venture on the Mississippi, it will be recalled, was by flatboat, and he notes from his own personal experience the danger and back-breaking labor of handling such vessels. When he returned to New England in 1825, however, he went by steamboat, and he noticed with satisfaction not only the advantage in comfort of the steamboat over the flatboat, but the improvement which the steamboat had brought to Cincinnati and Louisville (377-78). Flint may conventionally lament the passing of the river-boat-men, half horse and half alligator; but there is no doubt at all in his mind that the steamboat represents an unqualified improvement over the earlier and, however picturesque, more primitive methods of transportation.

The *Recollections,* in sum, is double in its purpose. It recalls not only a venture through the Wild West, but also the growth of what Flint considers civilization in what he saw as originally a primitive and barbarous wilderness. His extended description of the growth of Cincinnati will make the point clearer:

> Eleven years since, this was the only place that could properly be called a town, on the course of the Ohio and Mississippi, from Steubenville to Natchez, a distance of fifteen hundred miles. It is far otherwise now. But even then you cast your eye upon a large and compact town, and extended your view over the river to the fine buildings rising on the slope of the opposite shore, and contemplated the steam-manufacturies, darting their columns of smoke aloft. All this moving picture of wealth, populousness, and activity, has been won from the wilderness within forty years. In 1815-16 it contained between eight and nine thousand inhabitants, handsome streets, a number of churches, one a very large one,—a very spacious building for a Lancastrian school, and other public buildings, and two commodious market-houses. . . . While I am writing, it is supposed to contain between sixteen and twenty thousand inhabitants, with the increase of every appendage to city comfort, beauty, and opulence, in more than a commensurate proportion with its increasing population.

This passage comes at that point in the *Recollections* when Flint first sees Cincinnati. But it is obvious that his interest lies not in how this sleepy backwoods settlement appeared in 1815, but rather in what had been won from the wilderness in forty years—in the remarkable changes which had taken place in the town between 1815, when he had first seen it, and 1825, when he writes—and by implication in what would be done in the future. By putting such a description near the beginning of his work, Flint makes clear that the purpose of the *Recollections* is something more than mere reporting. His subject, he metaphorically tells us, will be the triumph of civilization in the West, and about this subject he has no mental reservations whatever. "It is a fund for proud anticipation," he says in conclusion to the passage quoted previously, "to minds that sympathize with the welfare of their country and of man" (37-38).

II *Histories of the Mississippi Valley*

Flint's next ventures in historical writing were to be much more ambitious than the *Recollections*. In *A Condensed Geography and History of the Western States* (1828) he attempted not only a history of the colonization of the West but a summary as well of all which was known in 1828 about its topography, fertility, climate, flora, and fauna; and to this he added predictions about its future growth and economic prospects. In addition, the book is filled with miscellaneous information of all kinds— remarks on the "antiquities" of the West, the fossil skeletons and mounds; the present-day Indians; the backwoodsmen and their customs. To this *Condensed Geography* Flint added a new second volume in 1832 entitled *The United States and the Other Divisions of the American Continent* and published the whole, after slightly revising the first volume, as *The History and Geography of the Mississippi Valley. To Which Is Appended a Condensed Physical Geography of the Atlantic United States, and the Whole American Continent.* The impression given by this rather grandiose title, that the important part of the book is the first volume, is certainly correct. Perhaps the publishers also wished to capitalize on the success of the *Condensed Geography* by indicating that the two books were more or less similar in scope.

Both books are conceived of as manuals, compendia of knowledge usable both by stay-at-homes in the East and by prospective emigrants. They are encyclopedic both in form and scope. Each begins with a topographical-historical description of the Mississippi Valley as a whole and then proceeds to a minute examination, by states and territories, of particular regions. This encyclopedic quality of the two histories limits their interest for the present-day reader, though at the time of their publication both books were very highly thought of. Flint seems to have visualized his own role in the publication of the books as that of editor rather than of author, and much of the material included in them, as he points out, is collected from other sources. In addition to collecting information about the West on his travels through it, Flint advertised continually in the *Western Monthly Review,* asking that those who had information about the West send it to him for inclusion in his histories. Much of the material which later appeared in these histories was first printed in the *Review.*

Though Flint feels no need to apologize for his scholarly qualifications as an editor, he does apparently feel that the subject of the West needs some justification. This attitude that some excuse was needed in order to write about the West at all, strange though it may seem to us, was quite important to him. Most of his later works begin with a prefatory statement justifying his subject, a justification which usually turns out to be eminently practical. Flint never sees much purpose in esoteric and occult researches for their own sake. If, as he suggests in the Preface to the *Lectures Upon Natural History,* "the open volume of nature" cannot show "traces of the finger of God" or "proofs, that divine love and wisdom are equally discernable in the great and the minute of creation," nonetheless, he consoles himself in the "Advertisement" preceding the first volume of the *Western Monthly Review* that "the future historian will repair" to his histories "as a synopsis, of most of what has been said and written, in the Western Country, touching its own natural, moral, and civil history." Not only that: Flint is certain that these "researches, touching the natural, moral, civil and geographical history of the Mississippi Valley" are "of public utility." His Preface to *A Condensed Geography* says much the same thing, adding a graceful statement that "a kind of affectionate feeling for the country" which "he had seen ... in some sense, grow up under his eye" had led him "to undertake this work." But again he tells us metaphorically that his real subject is more than a mere catalogue of facts. Not surprisingly, the subject of the *Condensed Geography* will be progress, and

Flint's qualification for writing it is that he was there to witness. He "saw the first steam boat, that descended the Mississippi," and "much of that transformation, as if of magic, which has converted the wilderness to fields and orchards," and he "wished to transfer to others some of the impressions, which have been wrought on his own mind by witnessing these changes" (I, 10-11).

In effect this statement means that, like the *Recollections,* both histories are conceived more as predictions of the future than as reminiscences of the past. The present is seen as a kind of way station to the millennium. As a result, both histories deal in predominantly predictive terms; and, by and large, Flint is a shrewd prophet of Western growth. He rightly sees the advantages of the fertility of Western soil, which he says is in general greater than that of the East. He mentions the abundance of mineral resources in the West and constantly emphasizes the economic implications of the geographic "fact" that the interior of America, from the Alleghenies to the Rockies, is bound together by one interlocking river system. He is outspoken in his advocacy of the development of canals, and realizes the importance of keeping the Mississippi open to free navigation for American ships. He understands that the primary problem facing the West is its remoteness from Eastern markets—an insight which is not particularly novel—but he also realizes, as many of his contemporaries did not, that this remoteness is more apparent than real, for distance in economic terms must be measured in time rather than in space. Flint understands that by water, with the aid of only a few canals, the West is open to rapid settlement and, once settled, both to efficient interior commerce and to trade with the Atlantic Coast.

The great drawback to Western prosperity, Flint sees, lies in the West's sparse population. An increase in numbers is necessary for economic growth. An increase in population means an increase in trade, as well as greater opportunity for Western farmers to sell their agricultural produce both near home and in Atlantic markets at prices competitive with Eastern farmers. It is interesting, by the way, to note that Flint's view of Western prosperity is implicitly based on the West's future agricultural expansion. He is not a prophet of Western industrial expansion, the possibilities of which he simply does not see. His orientation is consistently pre-Industrial Revolution. In the *Recollections,* for example, he describes Pittsburgh as a dying city, soon to be replaced by Cincinnati and Louisville. In terms of the economic geography of the eighteenth century he is quite right. Both Louisville and Cincinnati are nearer the center of the great inland river system of the Mississippi Valley than Pittsburgh is, and hence would inevitably become more important as trading centers. What Flint cannot anticipate—nor is there any reason he should be able to—is the change to be wrought on the whole economic structure of the Mississippi Valley because of the demand for steel brought about by the Industrial Revolution.

Since Western prosperity, in Flint's view, is directly dependent upon an increase in population, it is not remarkable that much of Flint's writing in the histories is openly directed at possible emigrants. Emigration, as he knew from his own experience, was not a step to be taken lightly, nor without some knowledge of the hazards it entailed. Most emigrants' failure to take hold was, Flint sees, the result of their lack of realistic anticipation of the demands which their new life in the West would put upon them. Flint never denies the immense cost in human suffering which emigration entails, but at the same time he knows full well that much of the emigrants' misery is avoidable. In the *Recollections* he mentions his first sight of emigrants in Cincinnati, sick from exposure, destitute and helpless. One family from Maine he found living in a single room, the father dying, the mother and three children sick with fevers. Though Flint comments that "it is gloomy to reflect that the cheering results of the settlement of our new states and territories, are not obtained without numberless accompaniments of wretchedness like this," he still realizes that the emigrants' predicament is in a large measure their own fault. The new settlers "were but too often wretchedly furnished with money, and the comforts almost indispensable to a long journey. It seemed to have been their impression, that if once they could arrive at the land of milk and honey, supplies would come of course" (40-41).

As is perhaps apparent from the above selection, Flint views the main dangers to emigrants as twofold. The danger of illness is everywhere, and parts of the histories seem almost intended to serve as medical comfort for the afflicted. Some of Flint's overwhelming interest in medicine is doubtless to be traced to his own ever precarious health, but much is due to other causes. The West did, in the early nineteenth century, have a reputation for unhealthfulness, and Flint often strives to refute unfavorable reports about the insalubrity of the climate. In the *History and Geography,* basing his argument on the census, he points out that the population of the Mississippi Valley has increased from one hundred thousand souls in 1790 to four million in 1830. Though he admits that some of this growth in population is a result of emigration, yet much, he points out, is also due to natural increase, and hence the climate cannot be too unhealthy (I, 135). But more heartening than these cold and rather comfortless statistics is the fact that the salubrity of the West is constantly improving. In his train the gallant yeoman brings not only prosperity but health. As Flint specifically mentions in *A Condensed Geography,* "it is a very trite, but true and important remark, that in proportion as the country becomes opened, cultivated and peopled, in proportion as the redundance and rankness of natural vegetation is replaced by that of cultivation, the country becomes more healthy" (I, 59).

This argument is not so silly as it sounds. Placing of swampland under cultivation, for example, was undoubtedly a major contributory factor to better health. Flint also hints that the Author of the Grand Design responsible for peopling the wilderness may have arranged things so that those who succumb to the diseases of a new climate are precisely those whom society can best afford to sacrifice to the demands of manifest destiny. In *A Condensed Geography* he remarks, as a kind of metaphor of the nature of colonization, that "in the productive and sickly sections of the south, allured by its rich products, and its exemption from winter, adventurers will successively arrive, fix themselves, become sickly, and it may be, they will die. Others, lusting for gain, and with that recklessness to the future, for wise ends awarded us by Providence, and undismayed by the fate of those who have preceded them, will replace them" (I, 199-200). Prudent citizens, the implication is, will wait their turn.

On the other hand, Flint reminds us in the *History and Geography* that even the prudent citizen might well "regard the salubrity of the spot selected [for settlement], as a consideration of more importance than its fertility, or vicinity to a market."

He should "supply himself with a good manual of domestic medicine," and, most important, should "obtain simple and precise notions of the more obvious aspects of disease," "have a lancet, and sufficient experience and firmness of hand to open a vein," "and above all, let him observe a rigid and undeviating abstinence from that loathsome and murderous western poison, whiskey" (I, 198). Under no circumstances should he consult the Indians, whose vaunted medical prowess was already becoming an unquestioned belief in American folklore.[5] Flint had "little faith in their boasted acquaintance with remedies, from their own vegetable kingdom," remarking that when "near our settlements, their sick are in the habit of applying to our physicians" (I, 128).

More important than the dangers of illness are the psychological dangers which the colonists must face. The assumption that going west is in itself a cure-all, an article of faith in which Americans still unthinkingly believe, Flint rightly sees as foolish. He himself had gone west not knowing quite why, expecting a land of milk and honey where supplies would come of course, just as in the histories he had pointed out that many emigrants had gone west under the same misapprehension. In the *History and Geography* he emphasizes that what he calls "imagination" is more important in influencing the desire to emigrate than even the emigrants themselves suppose. By "imagination" Flint means the common human failing of projecting our own desires as facts onto some fabulous big rock candy mountains somewhere in the West. "What mind ever contemplated the project of moving from the old settlements over the Alleghany mountains, and selecting a home in the west," he asks, without forming "new hopes ... of chasing down, in a new and far country, that phantom of our desires, always pursued in things without us [external things], and never found, except within us, happiness?" (I, 188).

The metaphor Flint chooses, that of hunting, is not accidental. He uses it a number of times in the same context, most strikingly perhaps in the *Recollections,* to point out that the *pursuit* of happiness goes more deeply into the American character than a mere figure of eighteenth-century rhetoric. "Very few ... emigrate simply to find better and cheaper lands. The notion of new and more beautiful woods and streams, of a milder climate, deer, fish, fowl, game, and all those delightful images of enjoyment . . . all that restless hope of finding in a new country . . . something that we crave but have not," this is the most common reason for emigration. The inevitable portion of one who goes west for such a reason is disillusion: "a few weeks' familiar acquaintance with the scene dispels the charms and the illusions of the imagination. The earth, the water, and the wood of these distant lands, are found to be the same well known realities of his own country. Hunting, though the game be plenty, is a laborious and unproductive business, and every thing visionary and unreal gradually gives way to truth and reality" (241-42). The seekers after the land of milk and honey will discover that it is no more than a land of dairy farms and apiaries.

But Flint goes on to say that, when the unreal advantages which the emigrant has imagined vanish into thin air, there still remains "a great balance of real and actual advantages in his favour," the most important of which, assuming the emigrant to be able-bodied, is that he "is forever freed from the apprehension of poverty." Flint has no sentimental illusion about the moral value of poverty or the ennobling effects of suffering: "Let philosophers in their bitter irony pronounce as many eulogies as they may on poverty, it is a bitter evil, and all its fruits are bitter" (248-49).

When the hero of E. W. Howe's *Story of a Country Town* begins his acrid appraisal of the American utopia by remarking "Ours was the prairie district, out West, where we had gone to grow up with the country" he is sardonically voicing a slogan which Timothy Flint would have accepted at face value. Flint could not have imagined a situation where such a remark would be made ironically. He could not conceive either that the country would not grow up or that, when it did, it would turn out in some way which he could not wholeheartedly approve. All around him were the evidences of prosperity: Cincinnati, won from the wilderness in forty years; Louisville, only recently the scene of Indian warfare, now transformed by the steamboat into a prosperous trading center; Wheeling, when he had first seen it a rude village, now turning itself into a city. This prosperity he traced in the *History and Geography* to "the onward march of American institutions" which, as they have protected her commerce and improved her cities, will foster Columbia's West-going sons:

> The greater portion of these immigrants, beside their wives, a few benches and chairs, a bible and a gun, commenced with little more than their hands. Their education for the most part, extended no farther than reading and writing, and their aspirations had never strayed beyond the desire of making a farm. But a sense of relative consequence is fostered by their growing possessions, and by perceiving towns, counties, offices and candidates springing up around them. One becomes a justice of the peace, another a county judge and another a member of the legislative assembly. Each one assumes some municipal function, pertaining to schools, the settlement of a minister, the making of roads, bridges, and public works (I, 192).

As her cities have grown, so have her citizens prospered; and this is the real theme of Flint's histories of the West. The affectionate feeling which he had experienced in watching the country grow up under his eyes he feels as well for those who have come west to grow up with it.

III   Western Monthly Review

When the emigrant arrived in the West and looked about him for a place to grow up with the country, one of the many things he was lacking was the advantages of polite literature. Indeed, he was lacking literature of any kind—many of the migrants, Flint had noted in his reports to the Missionary Society of Connecticut, did not even have a Bible; and Flint was not alone in assuming that without some medium at hand for the interchange of ideas and information the emigrant's present barbarous condition not only would not be ameliorated, but might in fact take a turn for the worse. Flint's belief in the progress of civilization through the growth of literacy and the possibility of free dissemination of knowledge, a belief tacitly held by most of his contemporaries, was for him not so much an article of faith as a program of practical endeavor. When first we hear of his determination to move his family West, one of his reasons for so doing is to found a religious newspaper, but one which, unlike the religious papers of New England, will "more particularly vindicate our literature, charities and institutions." Late in his life, he remarks in the *Knickerbocker*, in a long general article discussing the progress of humanity, that a new "intellectual era, second only in importance to that of the invention of printing, has just dawned." This is the era of "active and simultaneous effort to diffuse all that is useful in science among the people at large" (IV, 167). Most of Flint's literary endeavor is aimed at furthering the progress of this new era.

In the "Editor's Address" to the first volume of the *Western Monthly Review*, Flint addresses himself to the question of why a review is needed. He points out first that the Mississippi Valley may expect by 1830 to have four million inhabitants, but it will not have a single journal. It is self-evident, Flint says, "without our prosing upon the subject, that it is high time, amidst our improvements of every sort, that some effort should be made, to foster polite literature among us." The Westerner, he continues, has too long submitted to the intellectual tyranny and alleged literary superiority of the East; he should now stand up and be counted. "We are of the number," Flint concludes, "who are so simple, as to believe, that amidst the freshness of our unspoiled nature, beneath the shade of the huge sycamores of the Miami, or cooling the forehead in the breeze of the beautiful Ohio, ... other circumstances being equal, a man might write as well, as in the dark dens of a city" (I, 10).

A number of notions stand behind this rather belligerent statement. First in importance is the endemic American one that America has "listened too long to the courtly muses of Europe," as Emerson put it, and that Americans must find their own literary voice. The basic idea here depends upon a rather confused analogy. Since Europe, and more specifically England, is great, it has a great literature. If America had a great literature, it would be great too—or maybe the analogy should be put the other way round: if America were great, it would have a great literature. No right-thinking patriot could admit that America was not great; where then was its literature?

However loudly stated, such a remark as Emerson's masks a real feeling of cultural inferiority, one which was not confined only to American attitudes toward Europe, but which was also representative of the attitudes of more recently settled American regions toward those older regions claiming a fancied or real cultural superiority. When Melville, much more positively than Emerson, was later to say in praise of Hawthorne and in disparagement of Irving that "we want no American Goldsmiths; nay, we want no American Miltons," he was remarking on an international scale what Flint had noticed on a regional one—the quality of imitation in American writing which in some way not thoroughly understood muffles that original spirit which would doubtless put the forces of decadence to immediate rout—if it could only make itself heard.

It would have been almost treasonable to believe that the fact it cannot make itself heard is possibly because it is not worth hearing, and a corollary to the idea of unappreciated merit is the notion of willful malevolence. Just as the good citizens of the Mississippi Valley were later to suggest that their economic ills were due to manipulation of the world gold supply by a shadowy conspiracy of international malefactors, so was Flint to submit that the discouragement of Western literature was more than casually abetted by the hostility of the reviews. Not only the English but the American reviews as well are inexplicably negative toward new talent and fresh expression.[6] The *Western Monthly Review* will be different. Admitting that "in a young and growing community" writers will of necessity "be fresh and inexperienced," Flint promises that his review will take the role "of a gifted and good father developing the powers of a child, mixing discriminating praise with kind censure," or, changing the metaphor, "of an experienced and benevolent instructor, watching, encouraging, and enlightening the efforts of his pupil" (I, 16-17). Not that the nursery or the school will be either permissive or experimental; quite the reverse. "Show us an author," Flint says, "who advances an irreligious, or an immoral sentiment, an opinion that has a clear tendency to confound the unchangeable distinctions of right and wrong, unhinge principle, and overturn the social foundations, and we will do our best to paddle our skiff into the line of battle, and will fight with as hearty good will to the cause, as the best of them" (I, 14).

Flint's belief in the future of Western literature also rests upon the Romantic notion of the superiority of rural to urban life. What are the lays of artful Irving to the native woodnotes wild of the inhabitants of the nascent Mississippi Valley?

Combined with this almost Wordsworthian concept of the beneficial effect of nature on the creative faculties is an earlier, and for Flint a much more important, eighteenth-century primitivistic idea of the moral and physical benefits of the rural life. Flint's view of progress is ultimately much closer to Jefferson's than to Marx's in that, as mentioned earlier, it stops with the agricultural state. In the *History and Geography*, Flint had mentioned that one of the attractions of the Mississippi Valley was "that almost the entire population ... are cultivators of the soil." The urbanite, "whose daily range of prospect is dusty streets, or smoky and dead brick walls," though he "will have the advantage in some points over the secluded tenant of a cabin, or a farm house," cannot be "so healthy, so virtuous or happy" as the country dweller: "In striking the balance of enjoyment, the latter will be found to be the happier man, and more likely to have a numerous and healthy family" (I, 136). Since Flint's view of the creative process is implicitly non-tragic—however conventionally Romantic he may be in his nature-worship, he does not accept the other Romantic notion that an author creates works of imagination out of his own personal suffering—it follows as a matter of course that the good folk of the West, being both healthier and happier than the denizens of the smoky alleys of the East, will create a finer literature, if they just get the chance.

Nevertheless, if we look at the contents of the *Western Monthly Review* we discover that Flint's sanguine expectations for an immediate flowering of Western literature were not totally justified. Flint himself wrote at least three-quarters of the material in the *Review*, including almost all works of imaginative cast. The only major contributor of non-factual material beside himself was his son Micah, who regularly contributed poetry of rather good quality. The lack of more contributions of imaginative works was not too serious a drawback, however, since the *Review* was not primarily belletristic. Far the greater part of its contents was factual: material collected by Flint which would perhaps later appear in one of the histories; analyses of signs of physical development of the West, especially of improvements such as canals and railroads; anecdotal material dealing with the West; and finally, reviews of books, magazines, and government reports and documents.

The function of reviewing was one of the most important

purposes of the journal, and by far the greater portion of space was devoted to it. If the *Review* was to be an agent in civilizing the West, Flint rightly saw that one of the most valuable contributions it could give to progress was to make available in summary the contents of worth-while books which were almost entirely unavailable. The books which Flint reviews are of all kinds: journals of travel; reports of commissions set up to study the possibility of various improvements; novels of edifying, instructive, or historical tendency; works of divinity; books of political economy; and even an ambitious translation of the French *Dictionnaire Historique, ou Biographie Universelle*. To the present-day reader this material seems sadly dated, and he is likely to greet it with either a smile or a yawn; but its usefulness in 1830 cannot be overrated, since for the inhabitants of the Western states the *Review* served as one of the relatively few literary journals of any kind accessible in the West. In addition, it was the only one which attempted to be a forum for the internal affairs of the Valley.

In the three volumes of the *Review,* as well as the many factual items about the West which will be considered together in the next section of this chapter, are a half-dozen fictional works by Flint which are worthy of brief mention. Broadly speaking, they fall into two groups; sentimental tales and broadly comical sketches, almost slapstick in their humor. The first of the sentimental tales appeared in February of 1828 under the title "The Hermit of the Prairies." It details the fortunes of one Antoine Dardenne, son of a gatekeeper to a French marquis. One day Antoine saves the marquis' daughter (whose horse has run away), and falls in love with her. She of course cannot marry him and goes into a convent, where she eventually dies. Antoine learns from one of the sisters at the convent that she had intended to emigrate to America, and he sentimentally goes in her stead. Once in America he travels west and spends his life as a lonely hunter on the prairie where he undergoes terrible privations. He tries to forget his beloved, but is not always successful in doing so. When his grief becomes too strong, he takes a lock of her hair from his bosom and gazes on it and on her picture which he "bedews" with his tears, inquiring "why such harrowing affections, belonged to man" (I, 575). Finally, after years of grief-stricken wandering, he becomes religious and ultimately settles down as a hermit. After many more years of solitary life he rescues a young French lad from the Indians who, it turns out, is a grandson of the old marquis. The lad is named Marcellus—Antoine's beloved had been named Marcella—and the two of them become inseparable. They live together happily, but Antoine, who has been gifted with a sort of second sight, predicts the death of Marcellus. Sure enough, Marcellus dies, and Antoine then predicts his own death, which soon follows.

As can be clearly seen on the basis of this sketchy plot summary, Flint's interest in the tale has almost nothing to do with incident. The coincidences of the story are not only incredible—something which can perhaps be granted on faith as part of the necessary machinery for a romantic story—but in any deeper sense there is no "plot" at all. There is merely a series of random events. Weakness of plot was always one of Flint's great fictional failings, and in this story we can clearly see why: the story is simply an exemplum of a moral proposition. The proposition might be simply stated as the beneficent effect of religious consolation in assuaging grief. The young Antoine, deprived of Marcella, flees France and spends a melancholy life fruitlessly trying to drown his sorrows. He eventually discovers religious consolation, and this enables him to surmount the second great sorrow of his life, the death of Marcellus.

Though no one would pretend that this is one of Flint's best stories, it is in form emblematic of his artistic method in general. The "romantic" element of the plot—and Flint has been discussed far too much as a Romantic writer[7]—is of very little significance to the meaning of the story. It is a kind of window-dressing, a way of holding the reader's attention while a worth-while moral is given him. Consequently, though various clichés of Romantic machinery fill Flint's fiction—the lock of hair and the miniature which Antoine bedews with tears are good examples, as are the general habits of Flint's heroes of apostrophizing nature, of painting and sketching, and of moralizing at considerable length about the sadness of life and fickleness of fortune—they are relatively unimportant. They have almost nothing to do with what the story is about; they serve rather as a kind of shorthand through which Flint informs us that his characters are sensitive human beings, and by means of which he hopes to enlist our sympathies for them.

The story of "Agnes Sorel de Merivanne: The Recluse Coquette," which appeared in August, 1829, is also a fictional
exemplum of a moral proposition: the idea, crudely stated, that
a woman's place is in the home, and that the end of life is
matrimony. (This theme Flint was to explore later at full length
in *The Bachelor Reclaimed*, and it is always a basic attitude
in his fiction.) Agnes, who has lived for twenty years on a
lonely plantation near the Red River, has the unusual custom of
spending, twice a year, a night alone atop the highest adjacent
hill, from which she always returns the next morning plunged in
gloom. One day, she tells the reason for this strange custom to
a gentleman visitor to her plantation. She had been of patrician
birth, young and beautiful, but her head had been turned by
contemplation of her personal charms and she had "determined
to be the Napoleon of coquetry" (III, 59). Unfortunately she
discovered after a number of successful years as a coquette
that young men knew she was not interested in matrimony and
therefore refused to take her seriously. When her true love,
Lambert, was slain at Waterloo, she emigrated to America.
Up to this point the story is much like "The Hermit of the
Prairies," but a happy ending is brought about when Lambert,
the reports of whose death have been greatly exaggerated, returns
to her one night when she is praying atop the hill.

A religious metaphor is important to this story, as it was to
the earlier one, though it is applied differently. Basically, the
tale is about repentance for a wrong done. "The Hermit" is,
however, more successful than "Agnes Sorel." In "Agnes Sorel"
Flint allows himself to be trapped into a happy ending which
is totally gratuitous fictionally and completely unprepared for
philosophically. The tale has an offhand quality, almost as
though Flint does not realize that he is saying two things at once
which tend to pull his story apart. The major theme of "Agnes
Sorel" is the philosophical one that women are happiest when
married, and the ostensible point of the story is to detail Agnes
Sorel's discovery of this profound fact. But the story's other
theme, the theme of repentance, does not successfully reinforce
the first. "The Hermit of the Prairies" is much more successful,
for Antoine finally realizes both the tragedy of his mistaken
viewpoint and the pathos of his being unable to do anything
about it.

The final sentimental tale in the *Western Monthly Review* is much more ambitious than either of the other two. Flint thought well enough of "Paulina, Or, The Cataract of Tequendama," which appeared in March, 1830, to reprint it, slightly changed, as "Martha, Or, The Grand Cataract of Bogota" in the *Knickerbocker* in 1835. In the original version of the story Paulina is a beautiful young Colombian girl whose father, Don Pablo Isidore, takes into their home an American soldier named Gustavus H. Gustavus had been wounded in a sea battle when a Spanish vessel had attacked the ship on which he and Don Pablo were traveling. Paulina succumbs to the charm of Gustavus, but he is already engaged to an American girl back home. When Paulina discovers this melancholy fact, she leaps into the river just above the cataract from which the story derives its name, but Gustavus, now recovered, rescues her. Needless to say, the situation is a bit awkward, so Gustavus leaves for Bogota; there he finds a letter saying that his betrothed, "the fair Miss Sarah," has been "led to the altar by Henry Hunter, the rich, tailor-made, and essenced [well-off] capitalist" (III, 469). Gustavus returns to Tequendama to marry Paulina.

One theme of this story Flint had already developed at greater length in *Francis Berrian* (see below Ch. 4, Sec. I): the theme of the virtuous American's marriage to an exotic Latin girl. Here, however, the ramifications of the theme are not followed out. Paulina could just as well be an American as a Colombian girl so far as the plot of the story goes. It is only necessary that she be wealthy. The implicit point of the tale is to present the honor of Gustavus which forbids his acting expediently by marrying Paulina when engaged to another. The happy ending is not so completely gratuitous as in "Agnes Sorel" since it is at least within the realm of probability. In the revised version in the *Knickerbocker* Flint makes the ending more believable by emphasizing that the girl back home is a jilt and fortune hunter, a point which is only handled by implication in the earlier version of the story.

The comical sketches are on the whole less successful than the sentimental tales. The first, "Extracts from the Gazette of Oregon, Mouth of Columbia, July 5, 1900," which appeared in September, 1827, purports to be an account of the Oregon Fourth of July celebrations of the year 1900, but the real theme of the article is the triumph of the American future. The pretense of telling about the Independence Day festivities allows Flint to describe the improved comfort and standard of living in the America of 1900. In 1900 it is only a seven-day trip from Oregon to China, and this ease of transportation explains the large Oriental population of Oregon. Half the population of Oregon is Oriental, all are converted and "seem domesticated and exceedingly happy" (I, 256). California, lying to the south, is a happy Spanish republic. The West Coast of America is connected to the East by a network of canals, and to travel from the Missouri River to the Columbia is now only a twenty-day journey. Travel by balloon is also practiced, though Flint is vague about details. There is a general moral improvement in the tone of society, as evidenced by the conversion of the Orientals and the decline of religious disputation and sectarianism among the population at large. The sketch ends with a long, tedious, farcical description of an attempt to rejuvenate a Miss Emily Evergreen, age seventy-five, which enables Flint to poke fun at those who try to run counter to the immutable laws of nature and, more seriously, at the basis of folly common to all humanity, even the enlightened inhabitants of Oregon.

For all its attempted offhandedness and labored urbanity—at times the "Extracts" sound startlingly like Addison's *Spectator* essays—the theme of this sketch is one which is very close to Flint's heart. When he says, in quasi-apology for troubling the reader of the supposed gazette with trivia, that "after all, the records of the increase of comfort, and advancement in knowledge, morals, health, and easy and abundant subsistence, in private life, are a thousand times more interesting to the real friends of humanity, than all the heartless annals of power, politics and ambition" (I, 260), he is stating the one fundamental philosophical interest which is basic to all his literary production, fictional or not. The history of the triumph of the common man is the master metaphor, sometimes not explicit but always understood, of all his writing. It finds expression in his historical concern with the progress of democracy and the growth of the Republic; it is what determines his choice of literary heroes who, to his eyes at least, represent ordinary humanity; it is what informs his critical pronouncements, such as his praise in the *Western Monthly Review* for Sarah Josepha Hale, who "has discovered ... that a Yankee is as genuine a penny worth for a writer, as a daughter of the Incas" (III, 376), or his defense, in *George Mason*, of his own use of the subject of the common man:

> Of all stupid things in our world, it is the most stupid . . . that the great mass of readers should have thought, that there was no dignity nor interest in any adventures, but those of men that have fine houses and coaches. There are only a few hundreds of the former in our whole country. There are a million who can claim the alliance of kindred fortune with [George Mason]. The movements of human nature are just as strong in them, and if we would study them, would be found possessing as high an interest as those of the former (76).

George Mason, Sarah Josepha Hale's Yankees, and the Christianized Chinese at the mouth of the Columbia all represent to Flint one thing: the progress of America and the physical and moral improvement of its inhabitants.

It is not so odd as it might at first appear that Flint couches his predictions of American progress in the form of a utopia. Utopian thought has been implicit in America from colonial times. The citizens of a colony founded—as Governor Bradford, following scripture, assured them Massachusetts was—to be "a city ... set on an hill," might well be pardoned if they took the further scriptural injunction to "Let your light so shine before men, that they may see your good works" in a literary sense as an invitation to polemic; and, throughout American history, utopians have kept up a running fire on the progress of the city on a hill.

A case could be made for Flint as one of the early developers of the American utopian tradition, but to do so would overlook one important difference between Flint and the generality of American utopian writers. For from colonial times onward, American utopias have generally expressed a profound dissatisfaction with the American experience. Hawthorne's roughly contemporary analysis of Brook Farm, *The Blithedale Romance*, is a utopia turned inside out, and this is the main pattern of American utopian writing.[8] By the end of the nineteenth century, with the excesses of the Gilded Age, it was almost as difficult for writers to imagine America as a bona fide utopia as it would have been for Flint to have imagined it cynically. From the urbane skepticism of Howells' *A Traveller from Altruria* through the blood and thunder of Ignatius Donnelley's *Caesar's Column* to the wistful impracticality of Edward Bellamy's *Looking Backward,* the utopian consensus was that America was a noble experiment which had profoundly failed.[9] Yet Flint may perhaps be pardoned his innocence and capacity for wonder. When he looked about him America was in the process of quite seriously making itself into a utopia. Those who were not content to wait could join Robert Owen—whom Flint did not think much of—at New Harmony, or the Shakers, or the Rappites, or the Zoarites, or, later, the Perfectionists at Oneida or the Brook Farmers outside Boston.[10] Come when it might, the ultimate utopia was certain; and Flint can perhaps be forgiven for finding it at the mouth of Columbia in the year 1900.

"Jemima O'Keefy.—A Sentimental Tale," which appeared in November, 1827, is a burlesque of the sentimental story. It details the fortunes of Jemima, an American of Irish parentage, who meets Jacob Barndollar, a wealthy Pennsylvania German, and eventually marries him. In an Indian raid Jemima is carried off and held captive for five years by the Shawnees. Eventually she escapes and returns to Jacob, who in the meantime has married one Joan Windpuffer. Since Jemima is no longer wanted in Jacob's house, she returns to the Indians and marries a young chief.

The plot summary of this story gives little idea of the joke, which is a rather labored wheeze based on the notion of the invincibility of a woman of evil temper. For Jemima is a shrew, who succeeds not only in taming Jacob but in subduing the savages. Esthetically considered, the story is a failure, largely because Flint does not see the more general implications of his theme. To the modern reader, such humor as the story possesses comes from the jaundiced view of the progress of civilization inherent in Jemima's subjugation of two—in Flint's eyes at least—lesser breeds. But as Flint treats his material it has no satirical bite; he sacrifices the possible profundity of satirical treatment of his theme for the broader effects of burlesque.

"Violetta and Thoroughgrabb. A Tale," which appeared the following month, is even more obvious than "Jemima O'Keefy." It is a take-off, written in mock-heroic style, on what Flint considers the excesses of "polite" literature. It begins with a

Preface which rather too explicitly gives the joke away. The manuscript of "Violetta," Flint says, was anonymously sent to him; and he, in his editorial capacity, writes a straight-faced "puff" for it, saying that he has "seldom read any thing more affecting" (I, 441). The word affecting is not gratuitous, for affectation is the basis both of the broadly satirical style of the story and its plot.

The story takes place in the woods of Indiana, where Violetta, the daughter of a backwoodsman, lives in the family cabin built among the ruins of an Indian village. Her full name is "Violetta Lillietta Tabitha Killbear"—a rather good thrust at the pretentiousness of that frontier America which could soberly name a crossroads hamlet "Athens" or "Rome" or "Alexandria"— and she has the habit of reading Romantic novels. The point of the satire is now clear. Violetta tries to transform the crudities of rural life into the unreal pictures of her fictional guidebooks. She is courted by a country attorney named Jairus Thorough-grabb, and the courtship is described in flowery mock-heroic terms. The story breaks off at this point, after detailing the crudities of the country speech in which the lovers carry on their wooing.

It is difficult to understand why Flint thought well enough of this feeble tale to reprint it in the *Knickerbocker* in 1835, but one reason was almost certainly the fact that he felt the story served a corrective satirical function. Basic to the story are two common satirical themes which constantly appear in his other writing: the first, that the backwoodsman is much in need of civilizing; the second, that the stereotypes of sentimental fiction have no relation to life as it is. This second attitude is doubly presented in the tale. Violetta is enamored of life seen through the roseate glow of sentimental fiction, and her attempt to make life as it is agree with its unreal image forms the burlesque plot structure of the story. More profoundly, however, the style of "Violetta" attempts to ridicule that of sentimental fiction, and by implication to ridicule not only Violetta herself but also the readers of such fiction. Those who accept sentimental convention as true, Flint implies, would indeed find "Violetta and Thorough-grabb" affecting, but readers with a modicum of common sense will find it comical.

To modern readers one of the more disagreeable features of

"Jemima O'Keefy" and "Violetta and Thoroughgrabb" is the cruel fun poked at minority groups—the Germans and the Irish—and at the rude manners of the frontiersmen. It must be remembered, however, that Flint's attitude toward the various butts of his none too subtle humor is different from our own. He is writing what he considers to be satire—satire based on the old Horatian maxim of reforming manners by chastising them. Though he has no personal animus against any of the groups he pillories, he sincerely believes their ways of life to be inferior to his own. The frontiersman is removed by his isolation from the benefits of society, and the immigrant has not yet fully assimilated superior American ways. To aid in the process of assimilation is the specific purpose of Flint's satire, just as it is one of the larger general purposes of the *Western Monthly Review*.

The *Review* served the Mississippi Valley for only three years. In 1830 it ceased publication. It had never made much money for Flint, and the amount of work required to edit it and to write most of its contents was far too taxing to Flint's health and took too much time from his other literary work. When he had begun the *Review* in 1827, he had been an apprentice writer who needed the opportunity offered by the magazine to find an audience. In 1830 the situation was quite different. No longer an unknown, Flint had written two much read and greatly respected books of travel and geography as well as four novels, the first of which at least had been widely distributed and critically well received. The *Review* itself had been well thought of. In 1829 N. P. Willis had praised its "good taste" and "chaste and perspicuous" style. Later he was to mention it again. "There was a Monthly Review at Cincinnati," he told the incredulous readers of the *Athenaeum* in 1835; but, lest this should prove too incredible he added by way of explanation that Flint "was a New-England man."[11]

IV A *Land of Milk and Honey*

It is possible to draw a unified picture of American frontier life from the disparate works mentioned above and, to a lesser extent, from other of Flint's writings—a picture which is not only interesting in its own right but fundamental to Flint's fictional view of America and to his biographical interpretations of the lives of the pioneers. In its broadest terms this picture showed a land unformed, in the process of becoming. The picture was often drawn in predictive colors for which the present served only as a rough sketch. The details were largely to be filled in by the beholder, but the grand design was clear.

The most important elements in this picture were the inhabitants of the West. Originally they had been a crude and boorish lot, though their lives had had a certain tawdry romance which might prove seductive to the unwary. The boatmen, for instance, half horse and half alligator, led a life "in turn extremely indolent, and extremely laborious; ... generally plentiful as it respects food, and always so as it regards whiskey," and it was no wonder that it might have "seductions that prove irresistible to the young people that live near the banks of the river." The lure of the wicked river, though deplorable, was not, after all, to be wondered at:

> All the toil, and danger, and exposure, and moving accidents of this long and perilous voyage, are hidden . . . from the inhabitants, who contemplate the boats floating by their dwellings on beautiful spring mornings, when the verdant forest, the mild and delicious temperature of the air, the delightful azure of the sky of this country, the fine bottom on the one hand, and the romantic bluff on the other, the broad and smooth stream rolling calmly down the forest, and floating the boat gently forward, present delightful images and associations to the beholders. At this time, there is no visible danger, or call for labor. The boat takes care of itself; and little do the beholders imagine, how different a scene may be presented in half an hour. Meantime, one of the hands scrapes a violin, and the others dance. Greetings, or rude defiances, or trials of wit, or proffers of love to the girls on the shore, or saucy messages, are scattered between them and the spectators along the banks. The boat glides on, until it disappears behind the point of wood. At this moment, perhaps, the bugle, with which all the boats are provided, strikes up its note in the distance over the water.

Alas, it is all illusion, "the image of a tempting and charming youthful existence."[12]

Such a life can prove alluring only to those who know nothing about it, and the future lies not with them. They want, to expand

Flint's final metaphor, not to go west and grow up with the country but to keep it and themselves young forever. The future lies rather with the emigrant, who may be found "beside the rivulets, and in the little bottoms, not yet in cultivation, ... rearing his log cabin." Though such a man may appear undistinguished, he is the hope of the future. Pass his home in two years "and you will see extensive fields of corn and wheat; a young and thrifty orchard, fruit-trees of all kinds." In ten years the log cabin will be gone and in its place will be a brick house, and its humble and unpretentious occupant, "who came there with, perhaps, a small sum of money, and moderate expectations, from humble life, and with no more than a common school education" will have been made "in succession, member of the assembly, justice of the peace, and finally, county judge."[13]

In contrast to the alternately indolent and frenetic boatmen, the emigrant is distinguished by constant hard work. His hand is always turned not only to the business of increasing his own personal fortune but also to public works of all kinds. He is a tireless builder of canals, in which endeavor Flint wholeheartedly supports him. "We have always been earnest admirers of every thing in the form of a canal," Flint flatly tells readers of the *Western Monthly Review*: "Our Utopia should abound in canals" (II, 459). They will bring prosperity to the valley by furnishing rapid, inexpensive transportation; and, all things considered, they are not too expensive to construct (I, 73-78). More than that, they are a positive addition to the beauties of the country: "No spectacle is so fertile in poetical conceptions ... as to see the canal boats slowly wending their way through our wild and fresh country" (II, 459). Of course, everything has its price. The utopia of canals will not appeal to everyone. The Kentuckian whom Flint had traveled with on his journey west might well find a land where "the wild water-fowls will soon have to range other skies, to find out new and unmolested and quiet woods and waters," where "every thing is hackneyed, trampled and laid open," where "the keen glance of cupidity and speculation" would "survey the same woods and waters whilom traversed by the *coureur du bois*," where "the loneliness of nature is every where laid open to the calculating power of statistics end enginery" somewhat less than overwhelming in its attraction. But there are consolations: "It diminishes our regret to recollect...that the domain of comfort and utility is increased" (II, 701).

The Western passion for public works is not surprising, as Flint perceptively saw, for the whole tendency of the pioneer experience is to teach people to work together. The rugged individualism which a later age applied to the West as a projection of its own inadequacies was not for Flint. Fortunately, such anti-social behavior was largely confined to the region across the wide Missouri where trappers might safely indulge it. There the mountain men could harm no one but themselves through their indulgence in "outlawry" and "avarice" and that "appetite for lawless, unrestrained, and unwitnessed roving" necessary to breed "a reckless confidence in their own prowess." Within the confines of society such behavior could only be disastrous, for "combined, or social labor always effects more, than individual and detached labor," a fact which "is not only matter of opinion, but abundant experiment."[14]

And this interdependence is by no means to be deplored; for, despite all its imperfections, society is much to be preferred to solitude. The fact inherent in human nature that "men must cleave to their kind, and must be dependent upon each other" is the greatest single hope for human progress. In a community "pride and jealousy give way to the natural yearnings of the human heart for society" and men "begin to rub off mutual prejudices. They meet half way, and embrace; and the society, thus newly organized and constituted, is more liberal, enlarged, unprejudiced, and of course more affectionate and pleasant."[15] This is particularly true in America, where many different groups combine to form a society superior to any one.

Whether because of his contact with society or, more probably, because of his yearning after it, the average Westerner, even in the woods, is an orderly and responsible citizen. Unlike his wild and woolly compatriots in the fastnesses of the Rocky Mountains, who have never been curried below the knees, or the devil-may-care horse and alligator combinations who navigate the Mississippi River, the average settler, though undeniably rough, is also undeniably a diamond. The wildness of the Wild West and the lawlessness of its citizens, Flint is always at pains to point out, have been much overemphasized.[16] The wonder is not how lawless the citizenry is, but quite the reverse. Flint

speaks from experience. In the *Recollections* he reminds us that
as an itinerant minister he himself had traveled thousands of
miles through the frontier settlements "under all circumstances
of exposure and danger." In all his travels he "never ... carried
the slightest weapon of defence" nor can he "scarcely remember
to have experienced any thing that resembled insult, or to
have felt ... in danger from the people" (175). It is true that
the manners of the backwoodsman, when tried "by the standard
of New England customs and opinions" might have elements
"that would strike us offensively," but these minor gaucheries
are more than counterbalanced by the fact that the Westerner
is "sincere and kind without professions" and has "a coarse, but
substantial morality" (178). Elsewhere Flint reminds us that
though "it must be admitted, that in the interior, there is a
perceptible ... roughness" which, be it noted, is attributable to
"people who are far removed from the bosom of society," yet this
"roughness" of exterior never completely masks a heart of gold
which shows itself in "open hospitality" and "honest simplicity."
More important, this kindness of heart is not gratuitous. It is
something fostered by the benevolent genius of Columbia. "There
seems to be a strong tendency in American laws and institutions,
to create docility and habits of peace."[17]

The prospects for improvement in the West were staggering
to the imagination. Not only were the colonists to prosper
through the development of agriculture and the improvement
of transportation, but the valley itself was constantly to grow
more bountiful. The healthfulness of the climate would be
improved by cultivation, and the productivity of the land
itself would increase. Even though cavillers might assert that as
a new country is settled the springs dry up and water becomes
scarce, and though in fact a partial study seems to give some
credence to this view, since "the experience of almost every old
settler warrants the fact, that innumerable springs have failed,
since the cutting down of the forests that shaded the hills,
whence they sprung," such gloomy pessimism is totally un-
warranted. First of all, the opinion of old settlers to the contrary,
the fact itself is debatable. Flint himself is of the opinion "that
the western streams are fuller and more lasting, since the
cutting down of the forests, and that the Ohio and Mississippi
carry more water than formerly."[18] But, even if the old settlers

are right, there is no cause for alarm. The "truth beyond question, that Providence has designed man for the civilized state"[19] carries the strong implication that it will not leave him in the lurch to starve in the great American desert. Such indeed proves to be the case, for "a fact equally new, beautiful, and unquestionable has been settled by experience, that the innocent labors of the cultivator call down the blessing of the sky upon the earth." In plain language, this means that "when the thousands of square leagues of dry grass . . . shall become the resorts of husbandmen, the granges, the hedges, the young orchards, the mulberry groves, forming a new alliance with the sky, will generate showers, arrest the clouds, and pour innumerable rivulets over all these green wastes."[20]

Since, to continue the above quotation, "between the husbandman, the earth, and the atmosphere there seems a sort of compatibility and contract, that the one shall till, and the others grant moisture and increase," it becomes a subject of curious speculation why anyone would ignore so clear a divine mandate. Some benighted spirits do, of course; among them are the pioneers, whom we will examine in detail in the following chapter, and the Indians. Flint grappled manfully with the problem of understanding the quirks of Indian character; but, for reasons inherent in his view of society and of the good life, he never really succeeded in explaining them successfully. Indians were, axiomatically, inferior to whites, as was evident in their refusal to accept superior white ways. Despite all attempts at persuasion, the Indian refused to be at ease in Zion; missionaries, philosophers, soldiers, and the example of honest yeomen had all equally failed in weaning him from a perverse love of the forest, "desolate, like himself."[21]

This fact was unquestionable; but the motives behind the Indian's incorrigible behavior remained mysterious, for all Flint's attempts to discover them. The problem was all the more difficult because the Indians were "a shrewd and intelligent race of men, in no respects, as it regards combination of thought or quickness of apprehension, inferior to uneducated white men."[22] But, unlike uneducated white men, they were incapable of improvement. They of all people should know that "savage independence and generosity, and gratitude and happiness, in the green woods" are figments of romancers who have never seen a live Indian; and of all people they should "never undervalue the comfort and security of municipal and social life, nor the sensibilities, charities and endearments of a Christian home."[23] Yet for some unfathomable reason rational argumentation was vain.

Take for example the Indian attitude toward religion. "Pious and devoted Catholic missionaries have carried their lives in their hands, have renounced all earthly hopes, and have lived and died among them, to carry them the Gospel" and "the Protestants have not been behind them in these labors of love"; yet the melancholy fact remains that "after the lapse of more than a century, scarcely an adult savage can be found, west of the Mississippi, who will pronounce himself a Christian." Flint himself had tried his hand at conversion and had "scarcely noted an instance in which the subject was not received either with indifference, rudeness, or jesting."[24] More distressing, he found that, though the Indians might "listen with apparent docility and attention to our expositions of our religion, our faith, and our hopes," they insisted on telling him in return "their own fables, their own dim and visionary notions of a God and hereafter," and they "exact the same docility and complaisance to their creed, which they yielded to ours."[25]

With such attitudes it is no wonder that everywhere the savages are dying out. They are cruel and intractable, as evidenced by their inability to live, without quarreling, adjacent to the frontiersmen, "generally a harmless and inoffensive race."[26] Only the wise policy of the United States government has kept them from long since exterminating themselves. It has protected them from their unholy desire for whiskey, and "is exerting a constant effort, to hold the tribes leashed in, and to prevent them from destroying one another." But, despite its best efforts, an unprejudiced observer will see that the government is powerless in the long run; for "it is as unchangeable as the laws of nature, that savages should give place to civilized men, possessed of the strength, spirit, and improvement of the social compact."[27]

When, let us say in 1900, the last mountain man has been driven from his den somewhere in the Rockies, when the last Indian has died or been converted, when the sea of grass with its buffalo has given place to the farm with its cattle, when canals and railroads have driven the wild fowl to other waters—then the millennium will be at hand. From sea to sea the prairies will be covered with waves of grain and converted heathens, and cities will stand where once savages prowled for scalps. But, as Flint reminds us in his *Recollections,* "man is every where a dissatisfied and complaining animal; and if he had a particle of unchanged humanity in him, would find reasons for complaining and repining in paradise" (248). Perhaps he may then ask himself whether he is indeed in paradise, or whether he has not made a desolation and called it peace.

CHAPTER 3

O Pioneers

FLINT'S THREE WORKS dealing with the settlement and exploration of the Mississippi Valley through biographies of specific pioneers and explorers are the books on which rests whatever present-day literary reputation he may have. These books are *The Personal Narrative of James O. Pattie, of Kentucky* (1831), *Indian Wars of the West* (1833), and the *Biographical Memoir of Daniel Boone* (1833). The first of these must be passed over briefly, since it is uncertain exactly what part of the manuscript is due to Flint; the second is largely repetitive of material printed in the histories and in the *Western Monthly Review;* but the *Biographical Memoir of Daniel Boone* is worth a more extended treatment.

The Personal Narrative of James O. Pattie, as the title suggests, is not at bottom a work of Flint's at all. Flint himself, in his Preface to the book, states that his relation to the manuscript is strictly editorial and that his "influence upon the narrative regards orthography, and punctuation and the occasional interposition of a topographical illustration" (26). It will be recalled that Flint not only had traveled with Henry Bullard to Natchitoches and probably as far as the Texas border, but had spent the years from 1826 to 1830 assiduously gathering material about the Southwest for his various histories. The inclusion of such material, Flint claims, constitutes his only tampering with the manuscript, and he strenuously denies that he, as a creative writer, has at all influenced the presentation of the *Personal Narrative.* For, he says, although "it has been my fortune to be known as a writer of works of the imagination, I am solicitous that this Journal should lose none of its intrinsic merit, from its being supposed that in preparing it for the press, I have drawn from the imagination, either in regard to the incidents or their coloring" (25).[1]

So much protestation may perhaps legitimately be viewed with suspicion, but Flint's purpose is to claim that the *Narrative* is sober history. Apparently he felt that its wildness gave a certain unbelievability to the story—he was quite right—which might make the average reader assume the story to be fiction unless Flint personally vouched for its truth. Though Flint gives a number of reasons in his Preface for accepting the *Narrative* as true—in his opinion, for example, it is perfectly within the realm of credibility, and he produces character witnesses for Pattie who avow his inability to utter falsehood—modern scholars have formed a rather low opinion of Pattie's veracity. Though W. J. Ghent, for example, writing in the *Dictionary of American Biography,* is almost surely wrong in suggesting that the *Narrative* was largely written by Flint—that is, if we assume Flint's admitted meddling with orthography and punctuation is not "writing" the story, at least in the sense of "making it up"—his further opinion that the *Narrative* is "to be classed as semi-fiction rather than history"[2] is certainly correct. The plot of the *Narrative,* a rehearsing of which cannot possibly capture its atmosphere of hairbreadth escapes and impossible derring-do, details the fortunes of an American expedition to Mexican territory in 1824-30. In 1824 the expedition, led by Pattie's father, Silvestre, had gone southwest to Taos and then to Santa Fe. After trapping and adventuring in New Mexico, the expedition had gone north—just where is a matter of some conjecture—and had eventually gotten to California. James Pattie had returned overland to the United States and had arrived in Cincinnati in 1830, where he prepared his *Narrative* and gave it to Flint, who, after editing it, published it in 1831.

To a critic of Flint, the body of the *Narrative* has little interest, however exciting it may be in its own right; but Flint's purposes in editing it, as he explains them in his Preface, contain some interesting information about his attitude toward the pioneers. Pattie, Flint says, is "a legitimate descendent of . . . the hunters of Kentucky, a race passing unrecorded from history." He thus implies a comparison between Pattie and Daniel Boone, one which is not really far-fetched, since the Patties had come from Kentucky, where the elder, a contemporary of Boone, had been a redoubtable Indian fighter. Flint's ultimate reason for detailing the fortunes of the pioneers, however, is not purely and simply historical. At bottom it is a moral reason, for "there is a kind of moral sublimity in the contemplation of the adventures and daring of such men." The moral lesson to be learned from a study of Pattie and his fellow adventurers sounds quite modern: "They read a lesson to shrinking and effeminate spirits, the men of soft hands and fashionable life, whose frames the winds of heaven are not allowed to visit too roughly. They tend to re-inspire something of that simplicity of manners, manly hardihood, and Spartan energy and force of character, which formed so conspicuous a part of the nature of the settlers of the western wilderness" (27).

To offer the general reader the opportunity to examine this "nature" is the implied reason behind Flint's publication of the *Narrative,* and indeed Pattie himself, whenever his account of his adventures rises above the mere retailing of various more or less believable incidents, does attempt to give an insight into the character of those who conquered the wilderness. The ostensible theme of the *Narrative,* directly stated, is the triumph of frontier ingenuity over various kinds of peril: Spanish chicanery, Indian cruelty, and natural disaster. But the *Narrative* has another concealed theme which Flint must also have found significant: for despite all his ingenuity, bravery, and hardihood, Pattie is constantly worsted. Though he wins every battle, killing grizzly bears and hostile Indians and surviving incredible hardships, he loses every campaign. When he stumbled out of the wilderness in 1830, he was just as poor as when he had entered it in 1824. His lean years had gone for nothing, except insofar as he had gathered the raw material for his memoirs.

The temptation to place Flint's own experience beside Pattie's is overwhelming, and the results are to a certain extent illuminating. For Flint had himself gone into the wilderness, and not until he had renounced wilderness life had he himself amounted to anything. Though those who go into the wilderness are necessary in a providential order to prepare the way, the future lies with those who remain behind. This theme, implicit in the *Narrative,* becomes the keynote of Flint's later views about the significance of the pioneer experience. Though we may, if we choose, imitate the pioneer virtues of "simplicity of manners, manly hardihood, and Spartan energy," to plunge off on a wild-goose chase after furs and Spanish gold would only be foolish.

Indian Wars of the West, which begins with a general geographical description of the Mississippi Valley, draws particular attention first to its rivers and fertility, and then to its immense growth in population. This first description is not gratuitous; it implies the whole theme of the book: the settlement of the West. This theme is reinforced by Flint's method of presenting his material. The subject matter proper of the book begins in the third chapter, where Flint gives an account of the English occupation of Fort Duquesne, from which event he dates the English settlement of the valley; and from this time on his emphasis is constantly on *settlement.* After the British occupation of Fort Duquesne came the settlement of Kentucky, and Flint describes the Indian battles around each pioneer "station" and the growth of these into towns and ultimately into cities. Boone is seen primarily as a colonizer, and attention is called to George Rogers Clark as the founder of Louisville.

The Indian Wars, in sum, are a chapter in the history of colonization, and in military terms the turning point of the wars comes when, in 1779, enough whites have settled in the West to mount aggressive war against the Indians. This increase in population frees the whites from the necessity of fighting on the Indians' terms, and means that none but the very outermost settlements are any longer prey to constant Indian harassment. Of course, once free from Indian harassment, the relatively unexposed parts of the West can prosper; and their prosperity brings with it an immense growth in population and a consequent increased ability to carry war to the Indians' country. At the beginning of *Indian Wars of the West,* small groups of whites are seen fighting for survival against overwhelming numbers of Indians; by the end of the book, the situation is completely reversed.

This fact emphasizes the philosophical point of the book, which is the superiority of a civilized to a savage state. The valley, Flint reminds us, could hold only half a million savages, but once placed under cultivation it could comfortably support millions. In other words, the savage state contained the seeds of its own inevitable decline whenever it might be confronted by a technologically more advanced society. And to Flint's eyes it is axiomatic that such a society has not only technical pre-eminence but moral superiority. For the Indian, in the recent wars, has been motivated by an inexplicable bellicosity, while the frontiersman asked only to be left alone. The wars have been, in sum, the result of intercourse between "a race more calculating, more wise, with ampler means . . . but without the instinct of gratuitous cruelty, or a natural propensity to war as a pursuit, with another race organized to the love of the horrible excitement of war and murder for their own sake" (36-37).

If we leave aside the psychological naïveté which duly noted the fact that the Indians "saw in every settler a new element to effect their expulsion from their native soil" (36.) and yet could explain their resistance only on the basis of a "natural propensity to war as a pursuit," we discover that Flint's method of present-ing his material does have a certain real merit. Though we may not agree with his view of the benevolent nature of the Grand Design which informs Western colonization, the very presence of such an overriding concept gives the book unity and removes it from the dangers of redundance and triviality to which all such material is inherently subject. The book never slips into a tedious rehearsal of the horrors of Indian massacres, or a repetitive summary of the attack upon and defense of one frontier household after another. Though the material Flint must use is largely anecdotal, he is very successful in minimizing the pointlessness to which such material is always subject. Flint's particular—as opposed to his general—views of the reasons for white military success and Indian military failure are sound, and the *Indian Wars* as a result is at least good narrative history, however poor philosophy it may be. He rightly sees the inability of the red men to unite against the whites as the single most important cause of their ultimate defeat. The reason behind the failure of Indian tactics is that, "though the savages generally manifest sufficient cunning, they appear to want combined thought; and seldom make use of one advantage, as a means of obtaining another" (67). When compared with the inoffensive backwoodsmen, in short, they do not understand the science of war.[3]

Though Flint's purpose in telling of the Indian Wars is not primarily to justify or to explain the character of the pioneers, such explanation is occasionally introduced. Flint includes capsule biographies of a number of the pioneers, and the general conceptual framework of the book is evident in these particular descriptions. Though Flint begins the *Indian Wars,* as he had the Preface to the *Personal Narrative,* with a vigorous statement of the moral value inherent in contemplating the lives of the pioneers, his true interest obviously lies elsewhere. Though it may indeed "never be useless to contemplate these images of stern self control, of sublime vigor and perseverance," especially by those "born in times and under circumstances tending to foster effeminacy and selfishness" (13), an intentional note of reservation is found in all of Flint's descriptions of the pioneers, lest the reader take their example too literally. First of all, Flint does not romanticize the character of the average frontiersman. Those on the frontier, he says, were "the usual mixture of respectable and worthless people," placed by Providence in a position where "even those desperate characters that had fled from debt and the laws, were of use" as a barrier between the frontier and the savages (108). That there were worthless elements on the frontier no one would deny; but Flint goes further and points up the fact that even the respectable elements, though worthy of our esteem, should not be the basis of our emulation.

For instance, James Harrod, the founder of Harrodsburg, who was "exactly fitted for the duties and calls" of leading a party of settlers to the West, was congenitally unable, once the West was won, to adjust to the new state of things. So dear to him was the way of life of a pathfinder that even "after this primitive state of things had all passed away, after he had obtained the commission of colonel, had a family, friends, and comforts of all kinds multiplied around him," he would still perversely "leave his house, and repair to those parts of Kentucky, that were still wide and waste wilderness abounding in game," where he would "remain . . . two or three weeks, secluded from the sight of every human being" and where, on one of these expeditions, he died (57-58). Daniel Boone himself—though "he stands at the head of a remarkable class of people, almost new in the history of the species"—is a man happy only "in a boundless forest, filled with game, with a pack of dogs . . . and a rifle on [his] shoulders" (50).

It is significant in this regard that Flint remarks the Indian nature of both men: Harrod has "the instincts of an Indian" (58), and to Boone "the Indian way of life is the way of his heart" (54). Here is the basis for Flint's mental reservations about the frontiersmen; for some unfathomable reason, they were a kind of white redskin. It will be remembered that Flint's notion of the inferiority of the Indians to the whites has almost nothing to do with any difference in the physical or mental endowments of the two races. Rather it is a cultural difference; the Indians will not accept the benefits of civilization.[4] Any white who voluntarily becomes an Indian must also have renounced these benefits for an inferior way of life.[5] How different from James Harrod and Daniel Boone is Judge Symmes, one of the founders of the Ohio settlements, for whom Flint's praise is unqualified. Like Boone and Harrod "he was unquestionably fitted in a high degree to become the foster father to a new colony," but his qualifications are different and specifically suited to the future requirements of the Western territories: "He possessed a sound understanding, great firmness of purpose, and was a man of industrious habits, and devoted to business. . . . He was a zealous patron of the industrious and enterprising." Moreover, Flint specifically points out that he "had not the slightest touch of the hunter and *coureur du bois,* which so strongly marked the first settlers of Kentucky and Tennessee [such as Boone and Harrod], in his character" (146). Here was a man whom Flint could wholeheartedly admire. With all the moral virtues of the frontiersmen, he had none of their defects. He was completely untainted with that "wild recklessness" which Flint mentions as the necessary price of frontier virtues (50); and he would support any man who was "sober, industrious, and disposed to exert himself" (146). Unlike Boone, who was robbed of his Kentucky holdings by unscrupulous men, Symmes lived in wealth; and, unlike Harrod, whose bones mouldered in some unknown spot of wilderness, Symmes had been buried with dignity and his monument served as an inspiration to posterity.

I Biographical Memoir of Daniel Boone

When Flint undertook to write his *Biographical Memoir of Daniel Boone,* Boone's life and adventures were not new literary subjects. In 1784 John Filson had written the first description of

Kentucke, as he titled his book, and as one of the appendices to that volume he had included "The Adventures of Col. Daniel Boon; containing a Narrative of the Wars of Kentucke." These "Adventures," which did not purport to be a complete life of Boone, only covered the years from 1769, when Boone first went west into Kentucky, to 1783, when the Indians had finally been utterly defeated and the territory had been made safe for white inhabitants. In format Filson's *Kentucke* bears more than a casual resemblance to Flint's historical works, specifically to the *Indian Wars. Kentucke* begins with a general description of the Western territory, mentioning—as Flint was later to do in greater detail—its geography, cities, rivers, and climate; and it ends with a prospectus of the future developments of trade, navigation, and agriculture. The life of Daniel Boone and several accounts of the Indians are thrown in with an account of the curiosities of the country as being of interest though not of much deeper significance; but the real purpose of Filson's book is obviously to encourage emigration to the West. This may be seen from Filson's inclusion of a table showing "The Stages and Distances between Philadelphia and the Falls of the Ohio" and an amazingly accurately drawn and justifiably famous map of the then almost unknown territory.

The adventures of Boone were written in the first person, the implication being that Boone had either penned the narrative himself or told it to Filson. Filson's actual personal relation to Boone is unknown; it is almost certain that he knew Boone, for Filson had moved from Pennsylvania to Kentucky, where he had bought large sections of land, after the Revolution; but it is equally certain that Boone's "Adventures," in the form in which they have come down to us, are totally the product of Filson's hand.[6] The implication that Boone had written the work was soon made explicit, however, in pirated editions, with one of which, at least, Flint may have been acquainted.[7] Flint often refers to *Kentucke,* of which he did not think too highly. In *Indian Wars of the West* he reports Boone's "great satisfaction at hearing any one read the flattering and rather exaggerated and sophomorical account of him, which, as original and authentic matter approved by himself, has already been incorporated in these pages. 'All true,' he used to exclaim. 'No mistake there'" (219-20). At one stroke Flint admits both his indebtedness to, and disapproval of, Filson's work.

Filson's brief account of Boone is not without interest today. Written in a straightforward, unpretentious style, and organized with a good deal of skill, it is still exciting reading. The body of the story consists of narration of Boone's adventures, but the story is prefaced and concluded by some general remarks, also purportedly by Boone, which attempt to give the narrative some philosophical significance. Filson has Boone begin his account of his adventures with this statement: "Curiosity is natural to the soul of man, and interesting objects have a powerful influence on our affections. Let these influencing powers actuate, by the permission or disposal of Providence, from selfish or social views, yet in time the mysterious will of Heaven is unfolded, and we behold our conduct, from whatsoever motives excited, operating to answer the important designs of heaven. In other words, Providence, by means of "influence" acting upon human curiosity, attracts mankind to do its will. Boone goes on to draw the specific moral:

> Thus we behold Kentucke, lately an howling wilderness, the habitation of savages and wild beasts, become a fruitful field; this region, so favorably distinguished by nature, now become the habitation of civilization. . . . Here, where the hand of violence shed the blood of the innocent; where the horrid yells of savages, and the groans of the distressed, sounded in our ears, we now hear the praises and adorations of our Creator; where wretched wigwams stood, the miserable abodes of savages, we behold the foundations of cities laid, that, in all probability, will rival the glory of the greatest upon earth (49-50).

This attitude, it is immediately apparent, is almost identical to Flint's later view of the nature of colonization, not only insofar as it regards the general superiority of the civilized to the savage state, but as it remarks the specific importance of the pioneers as those who prepare the way for a superior way of life which will succeed them. By implication, of course, this condemns as inferior their own way of life. Filson makes the point even clearer by having Boone himself notice that the satisfactions of the pioneer life are largely in retrospect, in the contemplation of the greater good to follow, a notion which Flint himself later developed in his treatment of Boone. Lest anyone might miss the point, Filson makes Boone conclude his narrative with a restatement of the theme:

> I now live in peace and safety, enjoying the sweets of liberty, and the bounties of Providence, with my once fellow-sufferers, in this delightful country, which I have seen purchased with a vast expence of blood and treasure, delighting in the prospect of its being, in a short time, one of the most opulent and powerful states on the continent of North-America; which, with the love and gratitude of my country-men, I esteem a sufficient reward for all my toil and dangers (81-82).

The point is rationally clear, if perhaps psychologically untenable. It is also somewhat too optimistic; four years after the publication of *Kentucke,* Filson, on a surveying trip, was scalped by Indians.

Kentucke contained most of the material about Daniel Boone used by later literary artists, of whom the most important before Flint is Daniel Bryan, whose *The Mountain Muse: Comprising the Adventures of Daniel Boone* was published by subscription in 1813.[8] This work is an epic modeled after *Paradise Lost,* and Flint once commented that in his opinion it had been "consigned very unjustly to oblivion."[9] Modern readers are unlikely to agree; the seven books of *The Mountain Muse* seem almost totally without merit, for they are pretentious in form, long-winded in diction, and ludicrous rather than sublime. Bryan's most striking feature as a poet is a habit of garrulity which completely destroys the simple directness of his model. Filson's terse description of Boone's escape with his companion from Indian captivity is told in one and one-half sentences: " . . . in the dead of night, as we lay in a thick cane brake by a large fire, when sleep had locked up their senses, my situation not disposing me for rest, I touched my companion and gently awoke him. We improved this favourable opportunity, and departed, leaving them to take their rest, and speedily directed our course towards our old camp, but found it plundered, and the company dispersed and gone home" (52). As he tells this incident, Bryan destroys the simplicity of the style for no apparent purpose:

    Boone, perceiving Sleep
Its death-resembling seal had deeply stamp'd
On every savage eye; . . .

. . . .

With gentle touch his slumbering Comrade wak'd;
And off with light and speedy steps they stole,
Through the anfractuous brake, in whose dark maze
They wandered on, till Night's dim-beaming lamps
In Morn's wide-flowing floods of flame were quench'd.
They then in haste to their old Camp return'd,
And found it plundered and their Comrades gone! (118-19).

A more extreme example is Filson's laconic description of the death of John Stewart: "Soon after this, my companion in captivity, John Stewart, was killed by the savages, and the man that came with my brother returned home by-himself" (53). Bryan renders this bathetically at great length:

    Fierce, yelling swarms of savage Caitiffs, armed
With bloody Hatchets, from their ambush pour'd,
And instantly encircling him, let fly
Their death-commission'd Weapons, and dislodged
The intrepid Stewart's life! His lofty frame
Upon the frozen moss, blood-smoking fell;
His full bright eye now lost its lustrous glow,
And that strong-muscled face, commanding grace
And animating smiles no more adorn'd.
His high-view'd heart, where generous valor reign'd,
Where patriot feelings warm'd the flowing blood,
And kindled aims of daring Enterprise,
In Death's cold gripe was still! No more to beat!
No more to feel! In puddles now,
The vapid fluid once with spirit warm,
His lifeless bosom's frigid cisterns fill.

. . . .

What though *all this*, since Angels mourn'd thy fall!

. . . .

Since God's own vivifying voice will lift
Again thy scatter'd ashes from the ground;
And from his Holy Bosom send thy soul
The renovated tenement once more
To occupy; when spirit-wing'd it shall,

To join the sainted Hosts of Heaven ascend!
And with PHILANTHROPY's seraphic Sons,
Who bled conflicting with the embattled bands
Of fell Barbarians in the bloody West,
Forever bask in brilliant beams of BLISS!
    Much the surviving Heroes mourn'd the loss
Of their magnanimous Colleague and Friend;
Boone's bosom intimate, and VALOR's pride!
Again their dwindled number was reduced,
And Boone and his brave Brother left alone,
By the departure to the settlement
Of their remaining comrade (125-27).

Though Bryan's poetic ineptitude may well induce a smile, it is possible to see in this selection what caused Flint to view him charitably. For, unlike Filson, Bryan attempts to go beyond the mere relation of the events of Boone's life into some emotional rapport with his subject. Whatever one may say in praise of *Kentucke*, its range of emotional stimulus is very limited; it appeals primarily to the reason. Boone's motivations and feelings remain unexplored. Bryan on the other hand attempts, however clumsily, to give us some emotional response to the events he is narrating, and in this attempt Flint wholeheartedly supports him. If the purpose of telling the lives of the pioneers is to lead the reader in some way toward moral perfection, as Flint assures us it is, then the best agency for so doing is exhortation.

Flint's *Sermon*, discussed in the first chapter, may be recalled here, as may a more pointed comment prefacing a selection from *The Shoshonee Valley* in the *Western Monthly Review* for December, 1828. Speaking of novels, Flint lays down the principle that they should produce "good and right feeling" through playing upon the "tendency of human nature" "to love, to shed virtuous tears, and 'to feel another's wo'" by means of "seizing the broadest avenues to all that is noble and virtuous in our constitution" (II, 419-20). These "broadest avenues," he goes on specifically to state, are the various emotions to which a novel may appeal, in distinction to the purely rational appeal of a work of morality.

In this light the long passage I have quoted from *The Mountain Muse* becomes of more than casual interest. The passage is threefold in its development. First comes the description of the

event, the death of Stewart; second is an attempt at presenting
the reader with some kind of emotional response to the event
by means of a description of the dead Stewart; third is a moral
explanation of the meaning of the event. To Flint's way of
thinking, the "moral" of the incident, that Stewart—who has
died as one of God's soldiers in the great providential battle
to wrest Kentucky from the heathen—is now basking in brilliant
beams of bliss, can only be presented effectively by means of
making us respond emotionally to the pathos of his death.
Though Bryan may not in fact have successfully engaged our
emotions through the conventional *ubi sunt* he uses to portray
Stewart's death, he has nonetheless tried to do so and, Flint
would say, Filson has not. Filson contents himself with describing
the event and, at the beginning and end of the "Adventures,"
with stating that the events he has related have some larger
significance. He never attempts to persuade us emotionally of
the validity of the truths he is presenting.

Though a generation raised on Hemingway, to whom the
whole notion of "the sublime" seems more or less identical to "the
ridiculous," may well prefer Filson to Bryan on the *a priori*
grounds of a belief in the superiority of under- to overstatement
as a vehicle for conveying esthetic effect, such was not Flint's
view. To the bare narrative of Filson he hoped to add the
emotional power inherent in Bryan's poetic treatment of the
subject of the life of Daniel Boone.

Flint's own interest in Boone dates from at least as early
as 1825; for we find in the *Recollections of the Last Ten Years*
the offhand comment, significant in the light of his later writing,
that "the adventures of Daniel Boon [sic] would make no mean
show beside those of other heroes and adventurers. But ... this
Achilles of the West wants a Homer, worthily to celebrate his
exploits" (67). Flint's personal involvement with the fortunes
of Boone is even earlier than this: he had been acquainted
with Boone when both had lived near St. Charles in 1816, and
had known other members of Boone's family.[10] At first, however, Flint's interest in the character of the frontiersmen in
general—and of Boone in particular—seems to have been casual;
in the *Recollections* he mentions them in passing as being
interesting and picturesque character types and he conscien-
tiously notices and writes down the peculiarities of their

appearance and speech, but his account of them is no more than superficial. It is not until quite some time after the publication of the *Recollections* that Flint seriously turns to the pioneers as subjects for literary study.[11] The first issue of the *Western Monthly Review* (May, 1827) contains a sketch and description of "The Missouri Trapper," and in all his later writing the figure of the pioneer is very much in the foreground. In July, 1827, the *Western Monthly Review* contained one of Flint's few poems, entitled "Boon's Remembrances of Arriving in Kentucky," which, together with "The Missouri Trapper," forms the germ of the later *Biographical Memoir.*[12]

The *Biographical Memoir* is more ambitious in scope than Filson's "Adventures." Where the latter had confined itself to the period between 1769 and 1783, Flint recounts Boone's entire life, from his birth in Pennsylvania in 1746 to his death in Missouri in 1818. Since neither Boone's life nor Flint's treatment of it is generally well known today, a summary of the *Biographical Memoir* does not seem out of place. As Flint tells the story, Boone was born in Bucks County, Pennsylvania, in 1746. When he was three his family moved to Reading, Pennsylvania, and, when he was thirteen, to South Carolina. Even as a boy Boone was a precocious hunter, a point Flint makes much of by emphasizing the boy's love of wandering through the woods, by remarking how he killed a panther before his thirteenth birthday, and by telling an incident of how he put tartar emetic in the schoolmaster's whiskey, making clear the fact that Boone was not much, even at an early age, for book learning. When the family moved to Carolina, Boone became the hunter for the entire household, and Flint tells a charming story of how one night, when hunting deer with a lantern, he flushed not a doe but a young lady, Rebecca Bryan, a neighboring landowner's daughter, whom he later married. Pressed by the closeness of settlers on his heels, Boone again removed up the Yadkin River to the most desolate and isolated land in the Carolinas, where he met John Finley, who early in 1767 had gone over the Cumberland Gap into Kentucky and had safely returned later the same year.

Entranced with Finley's enthusiastic description of the new country west of the Alleghenies, Boone decided to settle there; and in 1769 he, Finley, and four companions prepared to start

out for Kentucky with the purpose of locating a suitable spot
for the new settlement. By June 7, 1769, after sundry adventures,
the little band reached the point to which Finley had penetrated
two years before, and there they camped. They found the soil
fertile and the forest overrun with buffalo, but Boone also
discovered "from innumerable circumstances which would have
passed unnoticed by a less sagacious woodsman" (52) that
the country was also infested with less welcome visitors—
Indians. Though "by a happy fatality" (53) they met no Indians
over the summer, the following winter they met with disaster.
The party had split up in order to hunt, and Boone and one
of his companions, John Stewart, were captured; after seven
days in captivity they managed to escape in the night—Flint here
follows Filson's account closely—and the next day met by chance
Boone's brother and another of the party.

Shortly after this incident, Boone and Stewart were again
surprised by Indians; and though Stewart was killed, Boone
managed to escape. The other surviving member of the party
then wandered into a swamp where he was torn apart by wolves,
leaving only the two Boone brothers isolated in Kentucky. On
May 1, 1770, the elder Boone himself returned to the Carolinas
for horses, supplies, and ammunition, leaving Daniel in Kentucky until July 22. Their only other companion, a dog, had
apparently had enough of privation, and went back to Carolina
also, leaving Boone absolutely alone. To keep from brooding on
the dangers of his isolation, Boone wisely went off on an
exploring junket to the northwest. Though once surprised by
four Indians whom he eluded by the strategem of swinging on
a vine in order to break his trail, and though once surprised
by a bear which he killed with a knife, he managed to survive
until his brother, riding one horse and leading another, returned.
The two brothers found a place suitable for their future home—
suitable, that is, once the Indians could be cleared out—and
then retreated to North Carolina, which they both reached
in safety.

From the time of their return to Carolina until September,
1773, the Boones tried to convince their neighbors of the desir-
ability of moving into the new land. By the end of September
they had interested nearly eighty people, their own families
included, and this party started off for Kentucky. On October

10, 1773, the settlers were ambushed on their way across the mountains, and six men, including the eldest son of Daniel Boone, were killed and a seventh was wounded. In addition, their livestock was driven off, and the party retired forty miles to the Clinch River settlement, then the last outpost of civilization. In June, 1774, the governor of Virginia asked Boone to go to the falls of the Ohio, above present-day Louisville, in order to bring a party of surveyors safely back to Virginia through hostile Indian country. Boone did so with a companion named Stoner, making the round trip, a distance of eight hundred miles, in sixty-two days.

During 1774-75 Boone was engaged in various exploring expeditions, the most important of which concluded with the construction of a fort at Boonesborough which was finished in June, 1775. In the late autumn of 1775, two years after originally setting out, the first party of settlers, including Boone's own family, finally arrived in Kentucky. Since the Indians did not attack immediately, the settlers became careless; and in July, 1776, the Indians raided the unprepared settlement. Boone's daughter and a companion had been "tempted imprudently to wander into the woods at no great distance from their habitations, to gather flowers with which to adorn their rustic fire-places," but such a love of the esthetic had proved dangerous in the wilds of Kentucky. The girls were carried off by Indians who were, however, chivalrous in behavior and treated them "with the utmost indulgence and decorum" (86). Taking advantage of this indulgence, the girls managed to leave a trail by breaking twigs and occasionally by leaving portions of their dress affixed to branches, so that Boone and a rescue party had no trouble in following them.[13] After fifteen days on the trail, the whites closed in on the Indian encampment; but when they inadvertently roused the sleeping Indians, Boone and Colonel Calloway, the father of the other captive girl, were taken prisoner. Sentenced to death, they were just about to be executed when the remainder of the rescue party attacked, defeated the Indians, and rescued all the captives.

At this point in the *Biographical Memoir* the scope of Flint's narration becomes wider. He has now demonstrated sufficiently Boone's superiority to the perils both of nature and of hostile savages, and Boone's cunning and bravery stand by implication as representative of the resourcefulness of the pioneers in general. Flint then returns to an outline history of the Indian Wars of 1776-82, material covered at greater length in *Indian Wars of the West.* He also describes details of pioneer life, concluding with a description of the construction of a "station" in the wilderness. He then details the greatest Indian offensive in Kentucky, the attack on Bryant's Station in 1782.

This short summary of Kentucky history, placed here in the *Biographical Memoir,* is a clever bit of organization. Flint has succeeded, half way through his biography, in universalizing his subject, and, by violating a strict chronological sequence, in giving a general background against which to play off the specific history of Boone. He then returns to Boone's particular fortunes and recounts his next capture by the Indians. In January of 1778, Boone and thirty men had set out for the Blue Licks (near present-day Cincinnati) in order to gather salt. Boone had been ambushed by two Indians and had escaped after killing them both—an event which, Flint points out to his readers, is commemorated in sculpture in the Capitol at Washington—but he was captured later by a large band of Indians on their way to Boonesborough, who also seized twenty-seven others of the thirty salt gatherers. Boone was adopted into the tribe of his captors—Shawnees—and remained their prisoner until they decided to attack Boonesborough again. He managed to escape and warn the garrison, which successfully stood off the Indian attack.

From this point in the biography the balance of power in the Indian wars has shifted in favor of the whites. Boone's fortunes are again played off against the larger picture of the punitive Indian campaigns of George Rogers Clark and, later, of Scott, St. Clair, and Wayne. From this point on white reverses in battle are not of any ultimate significance. The campaign against the Indians has been won, and later fighting, though bitter, is only a mopping-up operation. Although Boone's brother is killed by Indians at Blue Licks in 1780, soon after this the Indian menace is removed.

In 1780, Kentucky is divided into three counties, and Boone is made a colonel of militia. This organization of the "dark and bloody ground" into counties presages not only the coming of peace but also that of civilization. After peace is made, Boone again becomes a hunter but finds his range constantly curtailed by the settlers who move in around him. Though he had filed claims to a large area of Kentucky, he had not complied with all the legalities involved, and his claims were successfully challenged by later speculators. In 1792, Kentucky was admitted to the Union as a state; and this event, emblematic of the final victory of civilization over barbarism, sent Boone west to Missouri in 1798. When he passed through Cincinnati, he was asked "what had induced him to leave all the comforts of home, and so rich and flourishing a country as his dear Kentucky, which he had discovered, and might almost call his own, for the wilds of Missouri? 'Too much crowding,' replied he—'too crowded—I want more elbow room'" (237-38).

With this final removal, the story of Daniel Boone substantially ends, and Flint hastily gathers up in a summary the loose ends of his history. When civilization again caught up with Boone, he was living in Missouri, an old man incapable any longer of leading the van. He died in Missouri in 1818.

This skeleton summary of the plot of the *Biographical Memoir* should at least emphasize the interest inherent in its subject matter, and Flint exploits this interest with considerable skill. Flint is always at his best in description of events; and his treatment of the narrative, though more expanded than Filson's, never falls into the pretentiousness and bathos of Bryan's *Mountain Muse*. Boone himself emerges from Flint's pages as a believable character, a kindly and benevolent man as well as the predictable mighty hunter, resourceful woodsman, and cunning Indian fighter. Of all Flint's works, the *Biographical Memoir* is the one most immediately of interest to the modern reader.

Like *Indian Wars of the West*, the *Biographical Memoir* is more or less polemical in character, and the ostensible purpose of the two books is the same: to show the triumph of civilization through description of the winning of the West. Boone himself "in particular," Flint emphasizes, felt that his own efforts were part of a larger grand design. His personal interpretation of the significance of history was, Flint tells us, that "a firm and resolute perseverance had finally triumphed over every obstacle. That the rich and boundless valleys of the great west—the garden of the earth—and the paradise of hunters, had been won from the domination of the savage tribes, and opened as an asylum for the oppressed, the enterprising, and the free of every land.... he had caught some glimmerings of the future, and saw with the prophetic eye of a patriot, that this great valley must soon become the abode of millions of freemen; and his heart swelled with joy, and warmed with a transport which was natural to a mind so unsophisticated and disinterested as his" (226-27).

One should notice here that Boone sees himself in terms of a providential scheme; and he understands that his way of life, as well as that of the savages, will be eliminated by the advent of civilization. But, unlike his namesake in Faulkner's "The Bear," we do not finally see him laying futile claim to one tiny bit of wilderness for his very own. He is much more malleable to the providential design, for he knows that the garden of the earth has not been wrested from the savages merely to be turned into the paradise of hunters; the hunters as well as the savages must yield dominion to the enterprising freemen who will follow. Though this change will mean that Boone himself must constantly move on, he is fully conscious of his own part in the grand design, and, unlike the Indians with whom Flint often compares him, he resigns himself to the triumph of civilization.[14]

Flint develops the providential implications of the subject of Daniel Boone much more explicitly than do his predecessors. Though Boone himself, Flint assures us, is "contemplated in any light ... in his way and walk, a man as truly great as Penn, Marion, and Franklin, in theirs"—even though "he was not learned in the lore of books, or trained in the etiquette of cities"—this statement does not carry the implication that Boone is some village Cromwell denied by circumstance the opportunity for statesmanship which was offered to the three men Flint compares him with. Rather Flint's remarks carry an implied praise of the order which can place a man possessed of "a knowledge far more important in the sphere which Providence called him to fill" in that exact spot on this earth where his talents will do the most good. "Such a man was Daniel Boone," Flint goes on to say in order to make his point explicit, "and wonderfully was he endowed by Providence for the part which he was called to act" ([7-8]).

The point should by now be clear; Boone is of interest, it is true, in his own right, but his life is of philosophical significance only when considered in the light of that providential order which placed him in the wilderness. Though the hero of the *Biographical Memoir* may be Daniel Boone, its subject is greater than the fortunes of any one man. Its subject, in fact, is even greater than the historic settlement of the West; for, by contemplating the growth of Kentucky, late a howling wilderness, we may be enabled to arrive at some knowledge of the plan behind the providential order which directs the ends of colonization. Just as the ultimate purpose of scientific study is—for Flint—to enable us to arrive at some knowledge of the Divine order (see below, Ch. 5, Sec. I), so is the final reason for our study of history to provide us with some knowledge of the Divine purpose.

Flint's literary artistry lies in his very real ability to combine all these disparate "purposes"—the life of Daniel Boone, the history of the settlement of Kentucky, and the nature of the grand design which informs both these others—into a coherent and interesting narrative which is neither oppressive in its didacticism nor pointlessly anecdotal. His overall success is remarkable; and, even in particular short passages in the *Biographical Memoir*, his literary skill is clearly evident. As an example, consider this selection describing Boone's thoughts when he first hears Finley's report of the wonderful land of Kentucky, then unknown beyond the Alleghenies:

> In a region, such as Finley described, far in advance of the wearying monotony of a life of inglorious toil, he would have space to roam unwitnessed, undisturbed by those of his own race, whose only thought was to cut down trees, at least for a period of some years. We wish not to be understood to laud these views, as wise or just. In the order of things, however, it was necessary, that men like Finley and Boone, and their companions, should precede in the wilderness, to prepare the way for the multitudes who would soon follow (37-38).

The calmness of Flint's rhetoric should not cause us to lose sight of its cunning. The passage begins with a paraphrase of what very probably were Boone's immediate reactions to the description of the new territory; if they were not, they are at least fictionally plausible reactions. They recall Flint's own comments on the emigrant's hopes, hopes which, it will be remembered, are delusory. Boone wishes to escape the "wearying monotony" of his present life—farming—in order to "have space to roam unwitnessed," a desire he shares with the Missouri trapper, a character with whose motivations Flint was by no means in wholehearted agreement (see above, p. 18). Boone's wishes stand not only in explicit contrast to his present life of monotonous toil, but in implicit contrast to the lives of the multitudes who will soon follow him into Kentucky. By his remark that Boone's sentiments are neither wise nor just, Flint makes the point even clearer; and his next sentence draws us to the real subject of the passage: it is not Boone at all, but the nature of history. Flint wishes us to understand that what Filson called "curiosity" is used by Providence for its own ends. Yet, unlike Filson, Flint is not content with a mere statement of fact; he gives us, rather than a rational statement of Boone's point of view, a believable insight into the emotional nature of Boone's "curiosity," followed by an explanation of the purpose behind the providential order which could permit such "curiosity," which Flint has already deplored as in itself neither wise nor just.

To the modern reader, the most significant failing in the *Biographical Memoir* is the general lack of explanation of the nature of Boone's motivations. Flint can explain the attraction of Boone for the wilderness only on the grounds of an immoderate love of "indulging in his favorite pursuit.... the engrossing excitement of hunting" (229), which is a motivation that Flint never explains other than superficially. No emotional or mythic value is placed on this love of hunting, and as a result Boone's tragedy is ultimately only the tragedy common to all men, that of old age. When we last see Boone, he has resigned himself to the fact that he is too old to hunt; for he can no longer see his rifle sights, even when he fastens a bit of white paper to them in order to make their image clearer to his failing eyes. This insistence on Boone's love of hunting as sufficient motive in itself, however superficial it may seem to us, is not without some fictional justification. For one thing, it enables Flint to have his story both ways in regard to the most sentimental of all Boone's reverses, the fact that in old age he is cheated out of his Kentucky land holdings by unscrupulous speculators.

Flint unequivocally condemns the activities of the speculators as immoral and unjust; yet he points out in an interesting passage that they too serve the purposes of the providential scheme. Though Boone is understandably angry at being defrauded of his lands, his anger soon passes; for he reflects that he would no longer have been happy in Kentucky, "as it was ... becoming on all sides subject to the empire of the cultivator's axe and plow." Without much regret, therefore, he "sighed for new fields of adventure, and the excitement of a hunter's life" (236-37) and moved west to Missouri. What Flint has very cunningly succeeded in doing in his treatment of Boone's failure to keep title to his Kentucky holdings is to remove from the reader's mind any feeling of righteous indignation which he might have out of sympathy with Boone. Boone would not, Flint categorically states, have been happy in a civilized Kentucky; he would, therefore, have moved west to Missouri whether he had been cheated out of his lands or not. As a result, there is no need to waste sentimental pity on his plight.

What the modern reader is inclined to find unsatisfying in the *Biographical Memoir*—as in Flint's fictional or semi-fictional writing in general—is the fact that the moral choices are all too simple and too much on the surface. Flint never chooses to see the thematic implications of what might happen, given a younger Boone with the desire to hunt and no wilderness to hunt in; and indeed his purposes do not permit him to see such an implication. For Flint, the advance of civilization is an un-equivocal good, and he cannot permit the moral values implicit in a love of hunting to stand in even apparent opposition to it. He allows us finally to take nothing on balance: civilization must be an unequivocal good, and any apparent drawbacks it may have can easily be explained away. Other ways of life have nothing at all to be said for them, except insofar as they may perhaps serve a providential purpose; and the final cause of Providence, Flint makes abundantly clear, is civilization. As he treats the history of Boone's life, he not only can resolve the apparent equivocalities of the benefits of civilization into an affirmative statement but also can have Boone agree with his conclusions; for though Boone would not have been happy in a civilized Kentucky even had he owned it, as Flint specifically points out, he is now too old to hunt in an uncivilized Kentucky.

In opposition to Flint's view of the nature of the civilizing process, we may set that of James Fenimore Cooper's parallel study in the Leatherstocking Tales. The subject of both men is the same: an examination of the progress of civilization. The figures of Cooper's Natty Bumppo and of Flint's Daniel Boone are certainly comparable; they may even have been based on a common source.[15] Yet the themes of the two works are vastly different, and to the modern reader Cooper's is much the more profound. Where Flint's theme is the triumph of civilization, Cooper's is the price one must pay for progress. Whether or not Cooper believes that civilization is ultimately a development for good or ill, it must be taken on balance; and, from Natty Bumppo's point of view, it is a personal disaster.[16] Though Natty may be a providential servant, he is an unwilling one, and his view of history is sad. The grand design has killed his friends, has dispersed those whom he loved most dearly, and has driven him as an old man far from the wooded country he loved to spend an ignoble old age on the prairie. If this is progress, Natty Bumppo himself isn't having any; and he is man enough to say so. His heart does not swell with unsophisticated joy at the contemplation of the abodes of the freemen who have driven him from his home: In *The Prairie* he trenchantly reminds Obed Bat that the Garden of Eden "was not after the miserable fashions of our times, thereby directly giving the lie to what the world calls its civilizing. No, no, the garden of the Lord was the forest then, and is the forest now, where the fruits do grow and the birds do sing, according to his own wise ordering."[17]

Not surprisingly, Flint had little sympathy with Cooper, and his objections to Cooper's fiction may well point up his own attitude toward the theme of the civilizing of the West. First of all, Flint says, Cooper's fiction lacks truth; *The Prairie* has been written by a man with no conception of how a prairie really looks. Though "of all natural scenery, one would think, a prairie the most easy to imagine, without having seen it," yet Cooper is unable to depict it properly. "We shall read him with pleasure only, when he selects scenery and subjects, with which he is familiarly conversant."[18] That these remarks are imperceptive goes without saying; yet the inclusion of the word "subjects" gives us the real reason for Flint's objection. Not only are real prairies unlike Cooper's prairie (a fact which is more or less true), but, says Flint, Cooper's picture of the settlement of the West also lacks truth (a point which is much more debatable).

In another review, not specifically of the Leatherstocking Tales, Flint makes the same objection to Cooper's work. "Probability is violated at every step," he says; but more serious than this is the fact that Cooper's "stories have no moral aim—and leave an impression, perfectly equivocal, as regards their moral tendency."[19] Here is the heart of the matter. Not only should Cooper be read with mistrust because he has no firsthand knowledge of his material, but, more important, he does not know what his material means. Flint has no appreciation for the symbolic nature of Cooper's novels precisely because their "moral tendency" is equivocal or, in other words, because it runs counter to his own. It is impossible for Flint to conceive of anyone who would oppose the march of civilization for any reason other than willful blindness. History records the providential will, and there is no place for discord in the universal harmony of praise.

An age such as our own, which resolves its frustrations by projecting them into a fairy-tale past where they do not exist—a past where life was good because it was simple—can easily lose sight of the fact that Flint's view of the nature of Western colonization may have some small merit. "Roughing it" has always been a virtue appealing strongly to those who had the option not to, and pioneering is a way of life which is likely to be attractive to those who have never actually done any. Cooper's treatment of the theme of colonization is without doubt more profound than Flint's; his exploration of the nature of man and the ambiguities of life reaches depths which Flint's simple-minded optimism did not comprehend. Yet Flint's objection to the sentimentalizing of the frontier experience also has some validity. Cooper's notion of the realities of frontier life, Flint would say, is completely false; pioneering was simply not that way. Most pioneers would agree with him. An acquaintance of mine, speaking of a lifetime of labor as one of nature's noblemen, summed it up nicely: "It's a damn hard way," he said reflectively, "to make a dime."

CHAPTER 4

Novelist

F LINT'S CAREER as a historian and as a geographer began
in 1826 at the same time as his career as a novelist. Both
careers began with the publication of books well received by
the reading public; but from then on his two careers sharply
diverged. Although Flint's stature as a geographer and as a
historian constantly rose, contemporary opinion of him as a
novelist was never high; and, while *Francis Berrian* was often
praised, his later novels were received with relatively little
enthusiasm. The modern reader can easily get some inkling of
why, for the weaknesses of Flint's fictional writing stand out
clearly to one who has the hindsight of over a century. Basically
one might say that Flint's novels are rarely novels at all in the
most general modern sense of the word. Always excepting *The
Shoshonee Valley*, Flint's fiction is really not "fictional" in the
sense of being a work of "imagination."

Generally his fiction is written for one of two purposes: it is
a method of making historical events palatable, much in the
sense of the modern historical novel, except that its focus is
more explicitly on history itself than on the fortunes of the
hero who is witnessing the historical events being narrated; or
it is a vehicle for the exemplification of some moral truth which
is too often baldly stated by the protagonist. Needless to say,
both these elements, though they may logically be divorced
for purposes of explication, are closely bound together in any
one of Flint's novels, which as a result suffer from an excess of
didacticism.

This is not to say that novels ideally should not "mean" anything, but should in some way be their own meaning. It is rather
to suggest that the meaning of a novel should be in some way

greater than the overt statements of any one of its characters, even if his opinion may, for purposes of discussion, be taken as more or less "right." Put another way, Flint is unable in his fiction to present with any degree of verisimilitude the problem of "evil," chiefly because he has no real ability to present characters who disagree with his own philosophical positions (or who act in a way which he considers immoral) in any manner which might make their conduct explicable. Evil ultimately reduces itself to a series of unhappy incidents which thwart, at least temporarily, the good intentions of his heroes; the motivations of the man who does evil—or, indeed, of the man who acts in any way not in accord with the principles of virtue—always remain mysterious. Flint's inability to present motivations convincingly—a failing which we noted in the *Biographical Memoir of Daniel Boone*—always results in his fictional characters' being two-dimensional and hence more or less unbelievable as individuals. Consequently, though Flint's novels are full of excitement, they rarely have much drama; in any philosophical sense, the incidents are meaningless.

Flint himself was not unaware of this aspect of his fiction, and we must assume that he wrote as he did not so much because of inability to write differently as because of unwillingness to do so. When his biographer points out that in Flint's writing "the moral purpose is always in evidence often to the detriment of art in the story," and then remarks specifically that his literary technique depends upon his frequently stepping outside the story "to point out the moral, to preach and to exhort,"[1] he is not indicating a necessary evil in Flint's writing so much as a positive literary goal. For Flint was rarely concerned with purely "literary" values, as his remarks about the lack of moral tendency in Cooper's fiction should make clear. In his own novels he tends not to present an event but to preach about it, and he is not the man to make a sermon more effective by showing the devil's point of view.

If, however, we do not ask Flint to conform to twentieth-century standards of proper novelistic practice, we find his novels more impressive achievements than the above comments would suggest. Contemporary literary theory strongly condemns didacticism not only on the philosophical grounds that a didactic view of life tends to be at least partially wrong-headed but also on the grounds of craftsmanship: it maintains that didacticism is a poor way to convince. Hence the modern author goes to great lengths to conceal his overt purpose except by the tendency of his whole story. Flint would not have agreed with this modern notion at all; the purpose of literature was, he thought, instruction; and the clearer the point of the story was, the clearer the lesson would be.

As a result the modern reader often feels that Flint is overly explicit in presenting the moral of his several stories, which consequently lack depth. His heroes are always stereotypes: so-and-so is trustworthy, loyal, helpful, friendly, courteous, and kind; and so-and-so else is obedient, cheerful, thrifty, brave, clean, and reverent. And the reader is asked to take these qualities on faith. Similarly, his villains are the simple reverse of his heroes, and one is asked to take their qualities on faith also. It follows that the inner conflicts of Flint's characters can have no real interest to the reader of today.

What then is the literary value, if any, of his novels? Why, except out of historical curiosity, would anyone bother with them? The answer to both these questions is, I think, clear. We ask of Flint, as of all didactic writers, not for studies in the development of character but for explorations, in terms of parable, of moral problems. The profundity of his moral vision must be our ultimate—though not our only—criterion for judgment.

Flint's novelistic career lasted only five years, from 1826 to 1830. In this time he wrote five novels: *Francis Berrian* (1826), *Arthur Clenning* (1828), *George Mason* (1829), *The Lost Child* (1830), and *The Shoshonee Valley* (1830). Each of these will be considered in order.

I Francis Berrian

Francis Berrian, Flint's first novel, is a long and more or less improbable tale about an American soldier of fortune who goes to Mexico at the time of the Mexican Revolution. It is told mostly in the first person by Berrian to a chance acquaintance, presumably Flint. Flint, who had first seen Berrian on a steamboat plying between Philadelphia and Baltimore, had been immediately impressed by his self-reliance and his quality of keeping to himself. Flint never had the chance to speak to him, but he later discovers, after he has traveled overland to Louisville, that Berrian is a passenger on the same steamboat on which he is descending the Mississippi. The two men fall into conversation, and it is not long until Berrian begins to tell Flint his life history. After this the tale is told completely by Berrian until, toward the end of the story, he gives Flint a bundle of letters (which he just happens to have about him) that were written at an earlier date by his wife, a device which Flint apparently thought would enable him to develop another person's point of view toward Berrian's character.

The artistic problem inherent in the first-person narrative is one which Flint never successfully resolves in *Francis Berrian*. Berrian, it turns out, is practically an epic hero; and it is a difficult thing, as Flint is uneasily conscious, to tell the story of such a hero from his own point of view without the narrative's sounding terribly much like bragging. More perplexing, though an epic hero can boast, a Christian one should be modest; but to make Berrian modest without sacrificing his candor is beyond Flint's artistic ability. Flint attempts to solve the problem by insisting on the story's truth and by making Berrian constantly deprecate his own importance, but it must be confessed that the end result is to make Berrian's "'umbleness" a little too reminiscent of Uriah Heep.[2]

Berrian relates to Flint his life from birth to the time Flint had met him. He had been born, like Flint, in "a retired village, not far from Boston" (I, 14); and he gives a long and rather immoderate praise of the virtuous nature of his upbringing. Though clumsily handled, this is not without artistic purpose, for it establishes at once the fact that Berrian is no harum-scarum boy or roughneck, but rather a representative of solid Yankee virtues, virtues which later in the story are to be placed in explicit contrast with inferior Spanish ones. Berrian had gone to Harvard from which he had graduated at nineteen, being naturally of scholarly bent. His parents had wanted him to become a minister, but he had "had too high an estimate of the sacredness of those functions" to follow their wishes; and, on the basis of the delusory picture of the delights of travel painted in books of voyages of which, he confesses, he was "delightfully fond" (I, 19), he decides, despite his parents' wishes, to become a wanderer.

This decision, Flint implies, is not one which a mature mind would approve, but at the same time he has taken great care to show that Berrian is not so much a wild youth as an immature one who does not understand what he wants. It follows that the story will detail the steps in Berrian's education, and it proceeds to do so. From the very outset of his Western excursion, Berrian finds that the glowing pictures in his travel books need considerable modification in order to bring them into some accord with the facts. He discovers that the river boatmen are not noble and heroic but rough and crude, and that the West—particularly the mouth of the Red River where, it will be remembered, Flint himself had spent an unpleasant time—is unhealthy and filled with mosquitoes. He almost turns back when he sees how horrible it is, but decides not to, the sickliness of the inhabitants apparently not being sufficient warning. He himself soon becomes ill and almost dies. In his misery he wonders why he ever went west in the first place, a question which the rest of the book attempts to answer.

It should be noted that Flint has described Berrian's fictional experiences in the West almost exactly in terms of that "imagination" which he saw as the single most dangerous false reason for real life emigration. But, as Flint reminds us, when the unreal advantages of emigration vanish, "a great balance of real and actual advantages" remain, most important of which is that the emigrant is "forever freed from the apprehension of poverty." The rest of *Francis Berrian* details Berrian's discovery of these real advantages.

When Berrian recovers from his illness, he joins a party going into Spanish territory to traffic for mules; but he himself goes as a sightseer rather than as a trader. After traveling for some time into the interior of the Spanish territories, the party splits up, agreeing to meet later at Santa Fe; and Berrian with one companion decides to spend some time with the Comanche Indians who have a village in the vicinity. The Comanches, who have just raided Santa Fe, have brought back a number of captives, the most important of whom, Martha Miguela d'Alvaro, is the daughter of the Spanish governor. She is being held for ransom by her captor, a brave named Menko; and she confesses to Berrian that he is falling in love with her. Berrian promises to help her escape Menko's clutches; when Menko carries her off rather than returning her as promised—and, to add insult to injury, steals the ransom money as well—Berrian pursues them. He rescues Martha after a knife fight with Menko in which Menko is killed and he wounded, and they make a run for Santa Fe in order to escape the possibility of recapture by the Comanches. On the trip Berrian falls in love with Martha, though she is betrothed to another, one Don Pedro Guitterez; but he resolves never to act dishonorably toward her. In one of the most unfortunate passages in the novel, Berrian tells Flint, who obviously approves, that he finally came to the resolution to "follow the leading of circumstances," so that the Spaniards might "see that a well principled, and well educated young man will never swerve, for a moment, from the conduct prompted by integrity and self-respect" (I, 100). Ultimately Martha and Berrian reach Santa Fe in safety. They are received with rejoicing, and Berrian is invited to stay at the house of Martha's family until he recovers from his wounds.

With this detailed incident of Indian captivity and rescue Flint establishes the pattern of the romantic plot of the story. From this point on Berrian is of constant service to Martha and her family, only to be badly treated in return until the resolution of the novel. The reason for this bad treatment is implied in Berrian's earlier remark: it is impossible for the Spaniards to understand that a young man could offer service out of disinterested integrity. He must, they think, have some ulterior motive and, judging from their own characters, his motive must be corrupt and selfish. Spanish distrust of Berrian's personal motives also finds expression in their vociferous distaste for all things American, as Flint makes clear. While Berrian is recovering from his wounds at the house of Martha and her family, the talk at one point turns to politics. Martha's family is staunchly royalist: all are "instinctive enemies to every form of republican government." Considering the fact that Martha's father is an office-holder under the Spanish crown, this is not unusual; but Berrian takes umbrage at the Spaniards' assertion that America, himself excepted, is "a nation of pedlars and sharpers, immoderately addicted to gain, and sordid to the last degree" (I, 103). Berrian will not take this slander lying down, and he replies with a long and what Flint considers moving speech about the superiority of American ways and the great hopes of the American future—a speech which silences, if it does not convince, his auditors, with the exception of Martha's betrothed, Don Pedro, who has taken a dislike to Berrian.

The modern reader may well object to the "make-the-eagle-scream" quality of Berrian's long harangue and say with justice that it is nothing more than a piece of demagoguery, but again Flint's intentions are better than his performance. For the great error of Spanish ways is that the Spaniards cannot see the truth of statements which go against their own prejudices. This is nicely shown in the fact that they can except Berrian from their low opinion of America and Americans without ever considering that their opinion itself might be in need of revision. To show them the error of their ways becomes one of Berrian's purposes. Berrian's own contrast to Spanish intolerance is shown in his willingness to attend Catholic worship, though the Catholic father confessor, an associate of the family, is not willing to go along with this live-and-let-live attitude. Berrian says that "my views of religious obligation, and my principles, allowed me to go certain, but not all lengths, in joining the ceremonies of their church," and this view wins Martha's approval (I, 98). Again Flint has stated a point of some profundity in a silly fashion. Berrian's objections to Catholic worship are to what he considers the superstitious forms of an unreformed religion, and his partial acquiescence represents how far he can approve of them.

By this time, the real metaphor of the novel is clear; the novel is about "prejudice" and about its ultimate yielding to the force of reason. The Spanish prejudice against Berrian is threefold: first, it is personal, for the Spaniards distrust Berrian's private motives; second, it is political, for they distrust his republican principles; third, it is religious, for they distrust one who by choice remains a heretic. For various causes the Spaniards will not see reason, and Flint makes the point that most of these causes ultimately come down to selfish interest. The two real villains in the book turn out to be Don Pedro, whose love for Martha is only lust and whose politics are a transparent excuse for his own self-aggrandizement, and Father Josephus, the father confessor, whose religion masks a lust for political power.

The story, in sum, becomes a treatise on education. Martha and her family are finally brought to see the falsity of those in whom they have put their trust and to accept instead Berrian's position, with all that it implies.

The rest of the story may be quickly summarized. Berrian accepts a position as schoolmaster with the d'Alvaro family after turning down a captaincy in the army because he will not serve under the Royalists. The party moves south to the Conde's country estate at Durango where Berrian occupies himself for a time with teaching English to those of the household who wish to study. In return Martha, who becomes his star pupil, teaches him Spanish. Suspicions against Berrian come to a head when revolt breaks out in Texas, and he ultimately finds the situation at Durango so unbearable that he leaves to join the rebels, after winning a long religious argument with Father Josephus. The rebels whom he joins are undisciplined and, though they win a few battles, are ultimately beaten when the Mexican revolutionaries desert their American comrades. The point here is not ultimately a jingoistic one; the Americans, we are asked to believe, are fighting, as is Berrian, for an ideal; but the Mexican revolutionaries are more or less cynical in their republican principles, as is seen in their bloodthirstiness and their lust for gain, of which Flint gives us numerous examples.

After a short stay in prison, Berrian is rescued by a band of Patriot irregulars and flees to the mountains where he hides out with an Irish servant named Bryan, an elderly German named Benvelt who had in pre-revolutionary days been one of the d'Alvaro household, and Benvelt's three daughters. After a long and sentimental sojourn in the mountains during which time Benvelt and two of his daughters die, the remainder of the party comes down from its mountain retreat. Matters have in the meantime taken a turn for the better for the Patriot cause, and Berrian joins the resurgent Patriot armies, after safely delivering Wilhelmina, the surviving Benvelt daughter, to the protection of a Methodist minister who is to take her to America. After a series of melodramatic adventures which we need not detail Berrian becomes a brilliant general in the Patriot cause, the Royalists are routed, and, in the climax of the story, Berrian rescues Martha from Pedro, who is about to marry her against her will. Her father is proscribed by the tottering Royalist government and all his property confiscated because of his alleged Patriot sympathies—a pointed comment on the perfidy of monarchies—but Berrian is reconciled to him and marries Martha, despite d'Alvaro's disbelief that anyone would marry her now that she has no fortune. Eventually the Patriots are completely successful, the monarchy is overthrown, d'Alvaro is given his lands back, and the grateful Mexicans vote Berrian "a pension for life and an extensive and beautiful estate in the valley of Mexico" (II, 244), on which he finally settles down.

The most annoying quality of *Francis Berrian* is its constant melodrama, a feature which always more or less disfigures Flint's fiction. Flint never sees when the point he is trying to make is clear, and hence he overstates it through various shocking incidents, all aimed at showing us Berrian's moral nobility placed in specific contrast to the perfidy of Don Pedro and Father Josephus. We are willing to accept the fact that, for the development of Flint's parable, Don Pedro and Father Josephus must be villains of the darkest die; but the purposes of the novel call for them to be public rather than private villains. Insofar as the one uses love and the other religion as means to attain their own personal gain, we find them believable and interesting characters. But Flint insists as well on pointing out that they are not only public hypocrites but private cowards, and conversely that Berrian is a paragon of both public and private virtue. As a result, Berrian rescues a cringing Father Josephus from a carriage accident at one point in the novel; at another, a deceitful Don Pedro, whom he has bested in fair fight, attempts to shoot him in the back. Incidents such as these, really nothing but barely concealed didactic lessons, could be multiplied almost indefinitely; and no one can pretend they do anything other than seriously weaken the novel.

But even when we admit all these faults, *Francis Berrian* still has much to be said for it. First of all, the larger purpose of *Francis Berrian* is to attempt an exploration of the nature of morality by means of examining absolute moral standards in a corrupt world. The omnipresent metaphor of "gain" is Flint's best symbolic device for handling this theme, and he exploits it with considerable skill. Don Pedro and Father Josephus cynically use the pretense of morality for their own personal aggrandizement; the Mexican revolutionaries fight only for division of the spoils; and even d'Alvaro cannot understand why Berrian would marry his daughter when she has no dowry. Love and honor, exemplified in Berrian's character, are symbolically types of absolute morality acting in a corrupt world, without hopes of personal gain. If a man is to act morally, he must by definition act disinterestedly. Of course in terms of the story moral probity also turns out to be the best basis for pragmatic action, so that virtue is not only its own reward but also a well-paying proposition. Flint sees this objection to the morality of his parable and attempts to answer it, albeit the answer is somewhat unsatisfactory. When he leaves Berrian at the end of their trip southward, he concludes the novel with the remark that "I was verging towards something like envy at the idea of the rare felicity that seemed to have fallen to his lot. But on the whole, I remembered how soon the great leveller, Death, will set all these things on a footing of equality, and every emotion of that sort died away. I returned to the retirement and obscurity of my own family, blessing God, that he had once more restored me to them in peace" (II, 284-85).

The point here is not wholly the conventional one that he who acts morally will be rewarded in eternity, if not in this life. In addition, Flint is emphasizing the meaning of his parable in a different way. For Berrian's happy marriage, which is based on an absolute moral standard of love, is what Flint finally decides represents his "felicity"; and, Flint concludes, this "felicity" he has also. The accidents of fortune, symbolized by Berrian's wealth, ultimately do not matter. With this conclusion Flint metaphorically answers the question he had raised in the beginning of the novel: What are the benefits of emigration? Just as the Mexicans have been educated to the rational value of American ways—as shown by the conversion of the d'Alvaro family to Republican principles and by their ultimate awareness that Berrian will marry Martha for "love" and not for money— so has Berrian himself been educated in the real values of emigration. The unreal pictures which filled the travel books he had read and his youthful desire for adventure have both given way to a rational view of the advantages of emigration. Like the real-life emigrant, he has been removed forever from the evils of poverty; and, more important, he has discovered that happiness can be found only within himself. His "imagination" has been reformed. As Flint puts it, rather too explicitly: "If happiness on the earth be not all a joke, a mere poet's reverie, it is only to be found in the shades of domestic quiet and affection. I have meditated, as a disinterested looker-on, all sides of ambition, and distinction, and wealth, and pride, and my feelings constantly return to the ark of domestic affection, as the only place where happiness can find rest for the sole of her foot" (II, 267).

Viewed as a parable, *Francis Berrian* emerges as a novel provocative in implication, if not skillful in execution; and many of the objections raised to its alleged philosophical weaknesses—its apparent anti-Catholicism, for instance, and its unrealistic view of the actual differences between American and Spanish culture—disappear.[3] For Flint has succeeded, better than in any other of his novels, in abstracting a symbolic quality from experience and in transforming the raw materials of history into the metaphorical statements of art. A brief consideration of the factual basis to *Francis Berrian* may make this clearer.

The most important single source for *Francis Berrian* are the adventures of Flint's close friend Henry Adams Bullard, to whom the book is dedicated. As a young man Bullard had gone west and joined with a Mexican revolutionary general named Toledo, who had led an abortive revolt in 1813. Bullard had been a secretary and aide to Toledo, positions which Berrian holds in the novel; and Bullard had participated in the disastrous battle near San Antonio in 1813 in which the rebels were crushed by the Royalist forces. This battle is described in great detail, obviously from Bullard's own recollections, in *Francis Berrian*. Flint has combined Bullard's adventures with an account of the Mexican Revolution which overthrew Emperor Iturbide in 1823, and has telescoped the account of the two revolts into one.

Bullard's life is a source for *Francis Berrian* in a larger sense than this merely anecdotal one, however, and the novel can be read as a friendly tribute to him. In a general way Bullard's life follows the pattern of Francis Berrian's, and Flint's complimentary view of Berrian may well reflect on Bullard. Like Berrian, Bullard was a good student—both had graduated from Harvard at nineteen—and had gone west to grow up with the country. After his wild adventure with Toledo as a soldier of fortune, Bullard had returned to Natchitoches where he opened a law office, married, and became variously a judge, a congressman, and a professor. Berrian goes through the same steps as Bullard: he is first emigrant, then adventurer, and, last, a family man and a respectable citizen. In a more general sense this is the pattern of Flint's own life; and, as the remarks in this study should have made clear by now, it represents a course of action of which Flint highly approved. *Francis Berrian,* in sum, is not only a repository of anecdotes from Bullard's and, to a lesser extent Flint's, own lives, but is also a kind of composite symbolic biography of the two men's careers.

The anecdotal nature of *Francis Berrian* should not be overlooked, however, though the most intriguing anecdote in the tale comes not from the lives of Flint and Bullard, but, oddly enough, from the adventures of James Ohio Pattie, whom Flint was later to meet. This anecdote concerns Berrian's first meeting with Martha, when she is held captive by the Comanches. Martha, it will be recalled, is carried off by a brave named Menko and is rescued by Berrian, who returns her to her father in Santa Fe, where he remains as the family's guest. James Ohio Pattie, in his *Personal Narrative* (77-86), tells a very similar story. In November, 1824, Pattie says, the Americans in Santa Fe were awakened by an express messenger, who rode in "from the river Pacus [Pecos], on which the nobles have their country seats and large farming establishments, stating, that a large body of Indians had come upon several families, whom they had either robbed, or murdered. Among the number two Americans had been killed, and the wife of one taken prisoner, in company with four Spanish women, *one of whom was daughter of the former governor, displaced because he was an European.*"[4]

The Mexicans mount a punitive expedition which Pattie and his party join, and they catch up with the Indians on the fifteenth of November. The Americans ambush the Indians, who come up unaware following their prisoners, "women without any clothing, driving a large drove of sheep and horses." When the Americans open fire, the Indians kill three of the five women; but the two remaining, "one of whom was a beautiful young lady, *the daughter of the governor before spoken of*" escape. And Pattie, he informs us, bravely risks his life to rescue them. After a sharp fight in which ten Americans are killed and the cowardly Mexicans flee, the Indians are driven off. The Americans entrench themselves against the possibility of a surprise attack, when "the governor's daughter now inquired for the individual, who first met her in her flight from the Indians, and so humanely and bravely conducted her out of danger, and provided for her comfort." The next day they set off for Santa Fe, which they reach on November 17 and *where Pattie stays as the governor's house guest.* After a few days in Santa Fe, the entire party of Americans *goes to the governor's country estate as his guests* where they stay until November 30, after which they go off trapping and the incident is closed.

The similarities of the accounts of this Indian raid in *Francis Berrian* and in the *Personal Narrative* would seem to imply that the latter is the source for the former; but *Francis Berrian* was published in 1826, and the *Personal Narrative* was not published until 1831, nor, says Flint, did he know Pattie before 1830. How then can we explain the similarity of the two accounts?

Four possibilities immediately come to mind. The first—and least likely—is that the similarities between the two stories are coincidental. The melodramatic nature of the Indian captivity and the heroic rescue might well have occurred to both Flint and Pattie separately. Against this conclusion militate the striking similarities in nonessential detail between the two stories. The second possibility is that Flint made up the story for *Francis Berrian* and later interpolated it into the *Personal Narrative.* This seems unlikely to me on the basis of the more concrete and definite nature of Pattie's story. In addition to the fact that the lurid quality of the rescue by Pattie of a beautiful nude maiden is a kind of sensationalism which is totally absent from Flint's writing elsewhere, the account of the whole affair in the *Personal Narrative* is much more detailed than in *Francis Berrian*: the incidents of the ambush are specifically described by Pattie, while the details of Berrian's fight with Menko are told in paraphrase. On the basis of purely literary evidence the account in *Francis Berrian,* rather than that in the *Personal Narrative,* seems derivative and second-hand.

Third is the possibility that Flint had met Pattie and had heard the story from him, but this is most unlikely. The only time the two could possibly have met was during Flint's horseback trip with Henry Bullard early in 1825 to the *terra incognita* beyond Natchitoches. But at this time Pattie was nowhere around the Texas-Louisiana border; according to his own account, he was trapping in the Gila River country of southwest New Mexico. The fourth possibility, and to my mind the most likely, is that, while Flint was on his trip with Bullard, he heard garbled accounts of the Indian raid, accounts which probably contained only the outline of the events that Flint was later to hear in detail from Pattie—that there had been a raid on the Pecos River settlements in which the daughter of a former governor had been taken prisoner; that she had been rescued by a band of Americans; that they had returned to Santa Fe, where they had been hospitably received and entertained as guests by her grateful father. The news would still have been current at the time (January-February, 1825) when Flint and Bullard visited the Spanish settlements beyond Natchitoches. It seems more than an outside possibility that Flint's statement in the Preface to the *Personal Narrative*—that he can vouch for its truth because of "the reports, which reached the United States, during the expedition of many of the incidents here recorded,"—has particular reference to this specific adventure.

In any case, we know from the *Recollections of the Last Ten Years* that on this trip to the Mexican border Flint was turning over in his mind the possibility of writing a narrative about the adventures of Henry Bullard and the ill-fated revolutionary expedition in which he had taken part, though he tells his cousin James that this "must be reserved for another time, and a firmer hand." He mentions that he had already "collected some materials for the purpose" (372-73); and, though he gives no examples, the strong presumption must remain that the basis for the first incident of *Francis Berrian* was among them. In any event, when he returned from Natchitoches to Alexandria—and then to Salem—Flint had in hand all the anecdotal material which he later included in the history of *Francis Berrian*. A sign of his very real literary ability is that he could combine such disparate materials into a unified artistic whole.

II Arthur Clenning

The Life and Adventures of Arthur Clenning (1828), like *Francis Berrian*, details the adventuresome quest of a young man for his place in the world, and the story follows him from callow youth through romantic peril to a final resolution in domestic bliss. Unlike *Francis Berrian*, however, the book is not specifically concerned with the American westward migration, and it does not pretend to be factual in the same sense in which the former novel is. Though Flint opens the "Advertisement" to *Arthur Clenning* with straight-faced protestations of the novel's truth, saying that he got the manuscript from Clenning's own hand, this statement is obviously a literary ploy which is not to be taken seriously.[5] The real source for the novel is *Robinson Crusoe*, to which *Arthur Clenning* plays a long anti-primitivistic descant. But source studies of *Arthur Clenning* are relatively useless; of all Flint's novels, this one is most directly the product of the "imagination" of the author, unfounded in the world of external fact. And this "imaginative" quality of the novel, it should be added, does not always work to its esthetic benefit. Flint's own strictures on Cooper's lack of ability to describe something he has never seen might be turned against himself in this novel; for Flint is always more able to paint a scene which he either has known personally or has researched than a scene which exists only in his mind.

In one respect, then, *Arthur Clenning* is the most unsatisfactory of all Flint's novels; it is all at second hand, and the scene which Flint paints never succeeds in capturing our belief. This failure is partly due to philosophical as well as esthetic reasons, as will appear more clearly below. For to exemplify his philosophical theme Flint uses a metaphorical world in which he himself does not believe. Most of the action of *Arthur Clenning* takes place on a South Sea island, which for purposes of the story is a type of earthly paradise where the climate is always pleasant, where food comes easy to hand, and where living in general is effortless. The island, in short, is lifted straight from the never-never lands of eighteenth-century primitivism, and in this kind of land Flint does not personally have any faith. As a result, though the island serves a useful philosophical purpose, it is never very well visualized; the scene of the novel consequently remains abstract and bookish.

The plot of *Arthur Clenning*, much less cluttered with melodramatic incident than that of *Francis Berrian*, is simply told. Arthur Clenning is the son of a poor New York farmer. The Clennings have a tradition that they are descended from aristocratic Scottish forebears, and this makes them rather standoffish and nostalgic about their bygone blue-blooded connections. Arthur himself is a bookish lad, but his parents cannot afford the luxury of having one member of the family excused from work on the farm; hence Arthur, like Francis Berrian, sets out to seek his own fortune. Like Berrian, Arthur's first choice of vocation is a bad one: he determines to go to Scotland to seek aid from his aristocratic connections; accordingly, he ships as steward on a New York-to-Liverpool packet. Once in Scotland, he finds his relatives none too anxious to see him and, more to the point, he discovers that the family myth of wealthy and aristocratic relatives is nothing more than wishful thinking. Both sides of his family, the M'Allisters and the Clennings, are peasants—and poor. Flint's point is obvious, and is important throughout the novel: in order to succeed, one must help himself and not trust in rich relations or providential windfalls.

Arthur next decides to cast his fortune with the sea, and ships as steward on an East Indiaman, the *Australasia,* bound for the South Seas. His decision to run away to sea and become a sailor is much like Francis Berrian's similar decision to seek adventure in the Wild West, and Flint does not approve of Clenning's choice any more than he had of Berrian's. The desire for romantic adventure is one which both young men have to grow out of.

Aboard the *Australasia,* Arthur meets two young ladies: the one, Katharine Olney, is a prostitute being transported to Australia; the other, Augusta Wellman, is "the only child of a proud and disappointed courtier" (I, 44), who, with her father, is emigrating to New Holland to begin a new life raising merino sheep. One of Arthur's duties as steward is to make sherbet and lemonade for the female passengers, and, when he discovers that Augusta is drinking rather more than most of the other young ladies, he concludes "that in her caprice of taste, and wearied with her empire over the gentlemen passengers, she had made a study of him for the sake of variety" (I, 47). Arthur is proof against both her blandishments and those of Katharine Olney—a good ironic juxtaposition of which Flint is perfectly conscious—but, when her father discovers her attachment, he interferes, and she no longer comes for lemonade. The voyage continues fair until the *Australasia* passes Sumatra; then the ship runs into heavy weather. Eventually the *Australasia* goes down; but Arthur, as we expect, deports himself with almost super-human fortitude. What we do not expect is that both Katharine and Augusta are also brave, and Flint again makes use of the ironic juxtaposition to emphasize the fact that both girls are, appearances to the contrary, better than they seem. When the ship sinks, Arthur saves himself by clinging to a mast and is finally swept ashore onto a deserted island.

The next part of the book details Arthur's life on the island. Flint describes at great, if unrealistic, length the island's beauty, fertility, and kindness to man, and details Arthur's renovation of a cave for shelter, his discovery of oysters and breadfruit for food, and his explorations. But, at the same time, Flint emphasizes that the island is horrible without companions. He describes, in the most moving part of the novel, Arthur's growing desperation in his battle with loneliness. When Arthur explores the island, he cannot appreciate its beauty because he is alone; when he climbs to the top of a mountain, he sees that the island has no harbor, and that this means he must resign himself to a life of solitude; he tries to capture animals and domesticate them as pets only to find that they are too swift for him to catch; he becomes ill and has no one to nurse him; finally he convinces himself that others must have escaped the wreck, and so strong does this delusion become that he calls aloud to them:

> "Companion! Companion!" he cried, "I, too am alone!" He waited a moment almost in terror, as a thousand magnified voices answered from the mountains, "Alone! alone!" The deafening sounds seemed the reply of a thousand giants, that inhabited the caves of the mountains. He waited in breathless anxiety, till the remote reverberations, Alone! alone! died away, and his calmer reason convinced him, that these cries were no more than the responses of echo (I, 76-77).

This passage, if not original, is certainly effective in context, and Flint successfully caps it by having Arthur discover the wreck of the *Australasia*. He, like Robinson Crusoe, manages to salvage more than enough for his own needs from the hulk, but in a larger sense the discovery of the *Australasia* climaxes his frustration, for the only humans about it are dead. Arthur's search for companionship ends ironically in the discovery of the corpses of his shipmates.

At last Arthur, à la Robinson Crusoe, does find footprints; by following them, he discovers Augusta, who is ill with fever. He nurses her back to health, and they return to his cave which, luckily, has two rooms. Arthur soon finds, however, that even Augusta is not company enough; he then attempts to build a boat with which he hopes to escape from the island. Augusta, still the coquette she had been aboard ship, spends her time in domesticating animals, some of which Arthur has been able to capture after all. Her occupation has a double function in terms of the symbolic structure of the story. Just as she subdues the animals, so does she hope to subdue Arthur to her will. Even on the island, to change the metaphor, the artificialities of society have not given way to a more "natural"—that is, unaffected—way of life. But more important is the fact that Augusta, by domesticating animals, has created, for Flint's metaphorical purposes at least, a little society, and Flint contrasts the felicity of the captive animals with the incomplete lives of the isolated humans.

Eventually Arthur finishes his boat; but, when he and Augusta put to sea, they are caught in a storm, and return to the island, knowing their boat is too small for a long ocean voyage. They have a battle with cannibals, from whom they save a gigantic female captive, whom they name "Rescue" to commemorate the event, and whom they proceed to civilize. Since they have now apparently no hope of ever escaping the island, Arthur marries Augusta, whose coquetry has been shaken completely out of her by the second storm at sea. Rescue is witness to this impromptu ceremony, and Flint subtly emphasizes the fact that the germ of organized society now exists on the island. There is a family—Arthur, Augusta, and later their baby girl—as a symbol of the smallest human group which can make society possible; an outsider—Rescue—who symbolizes groups in society which are outside the family; and a code of law and custom—symbolized, on the one hand, by the marriage "contract" and, on the other, by the "civilizing" of Rescue—which makes possible the "social contract" both within and between groups. It should be noted that to Flint's mind the increasingly social nature of the island is an unqualified good. The restraints of law and custom which some would find an onerous burden Flint presents as an absolute necessity to human happiness. Just as Augusta's animals earlier had improved in felicity by exchanging their anarchic freedom for the restraints of domestication, so do the humans on the island increase in happiness as they move away from a solitary state toward a social one.[6]

Even with this germinal social order, however, Arthur still feels the need of society at large; and, when Augusta's baby is born, she too admits that they must make all efforts to leave the island. When they discover from Rescue that they are nearer to Australia than they think, they set off overland to the other side of the island to her tribesmen (Arthur, fearing that Rescue might desert them, has not told her that her own home is on the other side of the island; she thinks the cannibals had carried her a long way off). From there they eventually manage to reach Sidney.

At this point the novel again takes an ironic turn, for the society to which Arthur and Augusta have been singlemindedly trying to return for so long callously rejects them. The inhabitants of "Sidney's Cove" mock their connubial relationship as nothing more than fornication, and refuse to aid them. Finally a benefactor lends them passage money, and they return to England. There Augusta's father, who had also escaped drowning, denies them help unless Augusta abandons Arthur. His offer is indignantly refused, as is a later one by an ex-admirer of Augusta's named "Frederick B.," who offers Arthur "a considerable sum of money, on condition that he ... take the babe and embark with it to America" (II, 94) and leave Augusta to him. Eventually a series of benefactions enable them to go to America. They first return to Arthur's family in New York, but then strike out on their own and go west to Illinois, where prosperity awaits them. Arthur becomes a successful farmer, goes into politics, and the two of them are ultimately left a fortune by a repentant Mr. Wellman. Rescue, in a final scene of supposed comic relief, is to be married to Hurricane, an Indian. And all, we trust, live happily ever after.

The most charitable judgment one can give of the plot of *Arthur Clenning* is that the whole thing is silly. This silliness is probably due mostly to the fact that the plot is largely derivative. Even the sketchy summary above shows how closely *Arthur*

Clenning follows *Robinson Crusoe,* not only in general outline but quite often in specific detail: the fight with cannibals, for instance; the capture of Rescue; the removal of needed survival goods from the ship; Arthur's attempt to build a boat; his discovery of Augusta's whereabouts by means of the footprint he finds in the sand—all are interpolated piecemeal by Flint from Defoe's narrative into his own. Added to this is the fact, mentioned above, that the island itself is something which Flint can believe in only speculatively: given such and such an island, certain worth-while fictional themes can be presented. It does not follow, however, that the island has in any way to be accepted as even fictionally "true."

In short *Arthur Clenning,* like *Francis Berrian,* is a parable. In one way the similarity between the two novels is especially close, for both are ostensibly concerned with the metaphor of "education." In this respect the characters of Berrian and Clenning are more than casually comparable. Both begin as young men in search of the happy life, both attempt to find it by means of romantic adventure, and both finally discover happiness in wife and family. Similarly, the educational metaphor in the two novels applies to the wives of the respective heroes. For Augusta is brought to see the superiority of the values represented by America to those she has always held, just as Martha Berrian and her family are finally made to understand the superiority of American to Spanish values.

It cannot be emphasized too strongly, however, that the American values Flint symbolically affirms in both novels are not jingoistic, "my country right or wrong," patriotic value judgments. Though this fact is not so apparent in *Francis Berrian* as in *Arthur Clenning,* even in that novel it is evident that America is more a symbolic shorthand for a complex of philosophical notions than an actual geographic locality; and this usage becomes clearer if we examine those aspects of *Arthur Clenning* which set it apart from *Francis Berrian.*

Unlike *Francis Berrian,* which is much more personal in its drift, *Arthur Clenning* sets itself directly to an examination of the question of how man ought to live in society. That man cannot flee society for a primitivistic fairyland is given; how then is he best to live? The first alternative Flint examines is the notion of the "rich relatives" who will, Arthur hopes, enable him to live by removing him from the necessity of labor. The point is a symbolic one, and admittedly rather clumsily handled, but its meaning is clear: man must live through his own efforts. Rich uncles and the providential windfalls they symbolize are not to be counted on. Providence acts, if anything, in a different way; for whom the Lord loveth he chasteneth—and Arthur discovers this fact of life when the *Australasia* goes down. Once on the island he must work for himself in order to survive.

On the island he and Augusta Wellman discover their love, and this love plot again has a social meaning. For Augusta, a rich heiress, has herself attempted to live outside of society; she has been a "coquette" and has refused to undertake the social obligation of marriage and a family.[7] In terms of the parable of the book, the long interregnum on the island serves to teach both Arthur and Augusta the necessity for their coming to terms with society. Arthur learns first, and his constant endeavor while on the island is to discover some way in which he may leave it. Augusta is more unregenerate, and her education to the value of society in human life takes longer. First, she is made aware of the necessity of the family. Her marriage to Arthur marks her awareness that man cannot live absolutely alone, and that social intercourse in its very nature places an obligation on the parties concerned in it. Her education is not completed, however, until the birth of her child. Until that time society for her is limited first to herself and Arthur, and later to herself, Arthur, and Rescue. She does not want to go back to society in general until her child is born; then she realizes that the child's happiness depends upon a return to the outside world.

The importance of society to happiness is metaphorically shown in another way, which, as it is less didactic, seems more convincing to the modern reader at least. For as the conditions on the island grow to approximate the conditions in society at large, the lot of Clenning and his family becomes happier. When Arthur is alone, he is desperately unhappy; his felicity is considerably augmented by his discovery that Augusta too has survived the shipwreck; their felicity in turn is improved by their acquisition of Rescue and by the birth of their daughter. The implication is clear: insofar as their state approaches that of society off the island, it improves their happiness.

The reason for this effect, in Flint's view, is that a state of solitude is ultimately one of deprivation. Retreat from the world to a primitivistic paradise can never give more than a negative joy. Though Flint specifically mentions that "every thing that [was] painful and vexing in human condition, seemed to be abstracted from their lot" on the island (II, 7), he adds that the absence of pain is not the only condition necessary for human happiness:

> They had all that nature and love could supply. All this notwithstanding, they were obliged to confess to each other, that they wanted society. . . . They were obliged, amidst the solitary enjoyment of their groves, to admit how much men depend upon the common charities, decencies, small comforts, and almost invisibilities, and the influence of almost imperceptible relations, for a considerable portion of the sum of human enjoyment (II, 27).

The point is specifically made clear when Arthur and Augusta finally succeed in making their way to Australia. Among their first actions in "Sidney's Cove" is that of having their marriage made legitimate. Though this may well seem rather silly to us, Flint's point bears examination. They do not want the marriage legitimized for reasons which are either religious or even moral. Flint has already made the point clear that, in terms of ultimate moral questions, Arthur's and Augusta's vows, which they made directly to God while on the island, are perfectly sufficient. A conventional marriage ceremony is not necessary in order to secure God's blessing. But marriage has a social dimension as well as a religious one, and this dimension not only is legally important (an aspect of the marriage contract which Flint for his purposes chooses to ignore) but also is important to the happiness of the contracting parties. It is true that without divine sanction what is in Flint's view a legitimate marriage cannot take place; but, once divine sanction has been obtained, the social nature of the marriage ceremony contributes much to those "common charities, decencies, small comforts, and almost invisibilities" which Flint has previously mentioned as important to "the sum of human enjoyment." "When the ceremony was over," Flint tells us, "and in their retirement they embraced their dear babe, they felt how much the mind depends on the associations of publicity, solemnity, and the force of divine and human ties, sanctioned by public opinion in making up its estimates of things. Never had either embraced that infant before, without feeling an indefinable something that was wanting to the instincts of parental affection" (II, 63). As is perfectly clear from this passage, Flint believes that social approval is a necessity for happiness, though it is not the only necessity, nor indeed the most important one.

The "desert island" section of *Arthur Clenning* demonstrates the absolute need of society to human happiness; the final portion of the novel explores the question of how man may be happy in society. An uncritical acceptance of social demands is not Flint's final resolution; just as he had condemned the "affectations" of society as seen in the early character of Augusta, so he points out in the final section of *Arthur Clenning* that other values than mere social ones are necessary to happiness. For society, when Arthur and Augusta return to it, treats them badly. "Sidney's Cove" is cynically amused at their plight; London, the home of "affectation," demands that for acceptance they sacrifice moral virtue to social expediency; and Arthur's family in America, from which he had fled in the first place, is still too poor—in both a literal and a metaphorical sense— to support him without his working. He knew that "not an hour after" he and his bride arrived home, "there would be mental calculations . . . touching the difficulty of lodging, feeding and accommodating, such an additional number of people in their family" (II, 134). In short, Arthur has first to establish himself—a fact which he had learned on the island—and this must be the basis of happiness; to this basis social approval adds a needed further dimension. The resolution of the novel is again reminiscent of *Francis Berrian;* both men are happy and, in an etymological sense, "fortunate." But, though their happiness and their "good fortune" are closely related, they are not identical; and the distinctions between them are what Flint has attempted to present through the life and adventures of Arthur Clenning.

The most serious fictional drawback to *Arthur Clenning* is not to be found in Flint's handling of the parable but in the miscellaneous quality of the work considered as a whole. For, unlike *Francis Berrian,* the theme of *Arthur Clenning* does not really succeed in unifying the novel. The temptations presented by *Arthur Clenning* for miscellaneous preaching prove too strong for Flint's omnipresent tendency to moralize; as a result, great thoughts rear their heads throughout the novel like the cannibals on Arthur's island. Sometimes these concepts are only annoying, such as Arthur's predictable comment when he discovers the intact cargo of the *Australasia*: "How valueless was all this wealth and luxury to those unfortunates, whose bodies were stretched before him!" (I, 139); or the long marriage manual which introduces the second volume, clumsily concealed as a narration of the events of Arthur's and Augusta's honeymoon. Often, however, they are more serious. For example, there is the scene in which Arthur discovers the bodies of those wrecked in the *Australasia*. Among the dead is Katharine Olney, the beautiful London ex-prostitute who was being transported to Australia. Flint describes the scene as follows: Arthur has noticed the wreck and is making his way toward it, when "his senses informed him" that the ship is surrounded by the bodies of drowned sailors and passengers. "The next step, he started back with horror; for by the form and dress, rather than by the horribly disfigured countenance, he recognized the body of the lately beautiful Katharine Olney, the victim of lawless passions. Could it be, that this object of loathing and horror could have been the pursuit of illicit love, so beautiful, so interesting, even after her fall!" (I, 108).

What is unfortunate about this passage goes deeper than the priggish rhetoric used to state the thought. Here is an *ubi sunt* with a conventional moral, and one to which the pious could not possibly object. But though out of context this little Gothic exemplum is unexceptionable, within the framework of the novel it is not only gratuitous but spurious. It is perhaps true that beauty is only skin deep and that the basis of love should be interior virtue rather than exterior charms, but Flint's moral could be drawn from any corpse. Within the novel there is at this point no reason to distinguish between Katharine and Augusta on the basis of morality; both are concerned solely with the surfaces of things, and both have behaved courageously in the shipwreck, which can only imply that the interior virtues of both would develop through cultivation. Had Katharine been saved and had Augusta drowned, the same moral could have been drawn, with but a little alteration in the rhetoric.

Flint's most noticeable failure to see the implications of his theme comes in the handling of Rescue, whom Arthur and Augusta save from the cannibals. After they are able to establish communication with her, they discover that her home is on the other side of their own island. Flint somewhat naïvely tells us their reaction:

> They, of course, concealed these circumstances from her; for they saw such a strong current of feeling and tenderness in her thoughts and affections; such earnest and indelible remembrances, as, they feared, would induce her to escape, and fly over the mountains, if she were once aware of the little distance which interposed between them and her country. Uncommon quickness of apprehension, and great amiability of character, endeared her to her deliverers. She was aid, and society, and amusement; and her instruction and training were delightful occupations to them. Her loss would have been considered a great affliction and privation (II, 13).

Flint's candor here almost disarms us, and we have to think for a moment to comprehend what he is really saying. What he is saying is, we discover, nothing other than that kidnaping is justified on the basis of amusement to the kidnapers. In addition, when we consider the ostensible moral of *Arthur Clenning*—to demonstrate the incontrovertible superiority of the social to the solitary state—Arthur and Augusta's action becomes even more indefensible. Flint is apparently completely unconscious of any shortcoming here except for the fact that Arthur and Augusta have not had sufficient trust in Rescue's devotion. He concludes the passage by rebuking them for this: "They afterwards had the most ample opportunities to test the strength of her gratitude and affection, and to feel rebuked for their want of confidence in her." This makes matters worse, if anything; are we to conclude that, had Rescue wanted to return to home, family, and friends rather than be kept as a domestic servant by Arthur, his action would have been perfectly justified? This conclusion seems inescapable.

What has happened here, it seems to me, is that Flint has been so single-mindedly pursuing the "moral" to his story that he has lost sight of the fact that his characters are people as well as philosophical counters. He needs, in order to develop his parable, someone from "outside" to universalize the "society" which he has created on the island. To achieve this, he introduces Rescue; but he does not see that Rescue's own life away from Arthur and Augusta, if we believe in her as a character rather than as a personified abstraction, militates against the very moral he is trying to exemplify by introducing her.

In a larger sense, we may conclude, the failure to handle Rescue believably is symptomatic of Flint's major fictional shortcoming—his inability to create characters who are at once believable as moral types and as flesh-and-blood people. This shortcoming is not a major blemish in *Francis Berrian*, where the historical background of the Mexican Revolution tends to draw our attention away from the personalities of the characters in the novel; in *Arthur Clenning*, however, where there is no historical background at all and where there are only two major characters, it is a much more serious fault. We begin to grow restive when we discover that in fact we know nothing at all of the internal lives of Arthur and Augusta. Flint's habit of paraphrase, which in *Francis Berrian* draws our attention to the larger context of the novel, in *Arthur Clenning* succeeds only in concealing the characters from us. What we cannot hear, we also cannot see. After pages of dialogue in paraphrase between Arthur and Augusta—"Her preserver was instructed, that he must never for a moment forget, that the barriers, which had formerly interposed between them, still existed. He was to believe, that she viewed him with sentiments of inexpressible gratitude; that she had an entire reliance upon his honour and good principles; that she felt herself charged upon him, as a helpless being, who would increase his burdens, without being able to share his labours; who must be under daily and hourly obligations, in addition to the preservation of her life, and yet who saw no prospect of ever being able to make any adequate return" (I, 125-26) and so on and on—we understand what it is that we miss in *Arthur Clenning*. We miss direct perception of and participation in the lives of Flint's characters. We miss:

> "They look like white elephants," she said.
> "I've never seen one," the man drank his beer.
> "No, you wouldn't have."
> "I might have," the man said. "Just because you say I wouldn't have doesn't prove anything."[8]

III   George Mason

The history of *George Mason, the Young Backwoodsman*
(1829) is in a sense an extended commentary on *Arthur Clenning,*
though it turns for its subject matter from the never-never land
of primitivism to the Mississippi Valley Flint knew so well.
It is not so ambitious a work as either of Flint's two preceding
novels, and its philosophical aim is both much more simple
and much more directly stated. The moral purpose of the novel
is, we discover in the first pages, never to despair or, as the
subtitle of the book has it, "Don't Give Up the Ship."

The story does not repay the extended analysis given to
the novels discussed above, so a briefer summary and treatment
will suffice. The Mason family, consisting of the Reverend George
Mason, his wife, and five children, emigrates in 1816 from
New England to a settlement on the lower Mississippi River.
Not surprisingly an unreal view of the delights of the West has
influenced the Reverend Mason's move—he has been a reader
of "the romances of Imlay and Chateaubriand, and other writers
equally historical" (16)—and he has left a New England village
to taste the delights of the land of milk and honey. At first all
goes smoothly: a cabin is quickly built, game is killed, and the
family happily settles down around its own fireside. But the
Reverend Mason succeeds in offending many of his neighbors
who, though they have asked him to preach, dislike what they
consider his affectations of "cassock, surplice, and bands" (22);
and he also finds the work of farming too taxing.[9] He sickens
and ultimately dies.

In the meantime the two neighboring landowners, Mr. Garvin
and Mr. Pindall, who had originally been the Mason's benefactors,
have grown cool because young Pindall, who has fallen in love
with Mr. Mason's daughter Eliza, has been refused. (As Eliza
is only twelve, Mr. Mason thinks the proposal somewhat pre-
mature, but Pindall is not mollified.) The family has no ready
money, and the children are too young to operate the farm
profitably, so they turn to other expedients to make a living.
They turn entrepreneur, proceed to plait straw hats and to raise
silkworms. Both ventures prove profitable. Young George, the
eldest son of the family, is the guiding spirit behind these
enterprises; and, when the Pindalls threaten to foreclose the

mortgage which they have on the Masons' little homestead, George decides to become a clerk on a river steamer. This he does at a salary of $30.00 a month; but, being superior to the temptations which beset the ordinary boatmen, and industrious as well, his fortunes constantly improve. His wages are raised, he becomes captain and eventually half-owner of a steamboat, and ultimately he marries a girl he meets aboard ship who, it turns out, is rich. Eliza has also been removed from the threat of young Pindall, and she marries a Yankee whom she also had met on the boat and who is similarly well-to-do. At this point the story ends with a peroration to the moral "Don't give up the ship."

It is perhaps an injustice to consider this story as fiction at all. It is much more an extended sermon. In it, Flint's fictional situations, which always verge on the trite, are reduced completely to cliché; and the moral content of the story is similarly debased from parable to mere hortatory statement. This probably explains our lack of interest in the story, which is all on the surface and completely predictable. The device which Flint uses to hold our interest is so transparent that it fails to work after a few pages. The novel proceeds by means of presenting the Masons with some disaster which they overcome—only to be met by another disaster which they again overcome. When they are triumphant for the moment, Flint specifically calls our attention to the fact that they overcame whatever misfortune it may have been because they did not despair: They did not give up the ship.

Unfortunately, Flint's insistence on the moral of the tale eventually causes whatever conflict there is in the story to disappear. We become only too aware of the fact that, as long as George does not despair, he will overcome all his misfortunes. As a result, whatever "evil" there is in the story is made so impotent that we have no belief in it. George's refusal to despair is never shown in conflict with a situation in which he has to make the best of a bad matter. Consequently, his "morality" loses much of its force. Not despairing, we have the uneasy feeling, is not so much a moral imperative as a practical guide to self-betterment; George is a pragmatic man rather than a virtuous one.

Another problem with Flint's treatment of *George Mason* lies in the fact that he loses sight of the difference between "morality" and "good fortune" which he had distinguished in his earlier novels. Francis Berrian and Arthur Clenning are virtuous men who are also fortunate, but George Mason is a man whose virtue is aimed at gaining fortune, and this ambition gives his morality the spurious quality common to all heroes of his Horatio Alger type. Flint always has an unfortunate tendency to make his heroes, in Nietzsche's phrase, virtuous and paid besides, but usually he is able to distinguish virtue from its reward. In *George Mason* he is not, and the novel as a result is not only poor in execution but, when compared with his two earlier ones, superficial in conception.

IV The Lost Child

Probably the least successful of Flint's novels is *The Lost Child* (1830). Really not a novel at all, it is obviously a religious tract aimed at children, to whom Flint rather patronizingly refers throughout the work as "my young readers." The shortest of all Flint's novels, it has been overlooked by scholars until quite recently, and for a long time its very existence was problematical.[10] This confusion was at least partially due to the fact that the book was erroneously identified with its factual source, a short article in the first volume of the *Western Monthly Review*. The article tells of a true event of the winter of 1826-27, when a four-year-old child of a "Mr. Clark, of Hempsted county, territory of Arkansas" (I, 20), had been carried off by two horsemen. A letter of ransom sent to Mr. Clark was traced to the Natchez post office, and the mailer, Thomas Tutty, who had asked for $250 in ransom, was arrested and jailed. For a long time Tutty remained silent about the whereabouts of the kidnaped child; but, after sending law officers on a wild-goose chase to a house some fifty miles from Natchez, he was released in the custody of Mr. Clark, whom he agreed to take to the child's hiding place. On the way Tutty attempted to kill Clark, failed, leaped into the river, and drowned. The article ends at this point in the history of the child, and is obviously intended to publicize the story of the kidnaping in hopes that some further news of the child's whereabouts would turn up.

The novel faithfully follows the events of the story to this point and then goes on to tell of the recovery of the child, which took place after the article had appeared. Then it continues to tell how young "Henry Howe"—the child's name has been changed—was first taken to the hideout of the gang of robbers by Tuttell (the name "Tutty" used on the ransom note had been a clumsy attempt at disguise) and Callendar (the other kidnaper), then was carried farther off, and finally was left with another gang when Callendar and Tuttell, wanted on a murder charge, were forced to flee into the wilderness. The hardships of captivity cause Henry to become both mentally and physically ill, and though he eventually recovers his physical health, his mind is never completely restored. Ever afterward he is a victim of total amnesia in regard to the events of his abduction and captivity. Eventually the gang gives him to a pedlar, who is supposed to carry him down the Red River and lose him where someone will find him; the pedlar does so, leaving him with a woman in Alexandria, who in turn gives him to the wife of the jail-keeper. After two and one-half years the jail-keeper's wife is hailed into court on the charge of maltreatment of a child—namely Henry—and Henry is taken away from her and given to some kindly people. He is finally recognized by a friend of Mr. Howe's and is taken home.

In the meantime, Flint fills in the background of the story of Tuttell. After fleeing into the wilderness from the law, Tuttell and Callendar had split up; and Callendar, Flint parenthetically adds, is still at large. Tuttell, after the search for him has petered out, arrives in Mississippi, passes himself off as a schoolteacher, and succeeds in getting a position. His erstwhile criminal associates find him, however, and blackmail him, and this is what forces him to write the ransom note which eventually leads to his capture. (It should be added that this section of the book which ironically investigates the notion of "honor among thieves" is by far the most effective part.)

The story of The Lost Child is gripping enough in its own right, and had Flint remained content merely to tell it for its own inherent interest, the book would doubtless have been more successful than it is. Flint made the mistake, however, of clothing the story with a moral which does not quite fit. From one point of view, the story is focused on Henry, and his reactions are reminiscent of George Mason's. Throughout his tempestuous career Henry doesn't give up the ship, and obviously he wins Flint's approval for this. In fact, Henry is quite the paragon of Christian youth. In the beginning of the book we find him "intelligent and engaging in manner, of an amiable disposition, and affectionate to his parents and brother and sister" (15). When Tuttell and Callendar carry him off, Henry solaces himself by piously reflecting that "they cannot take away my Heavenly Father" (55); and, as a sadder and presumably wiser child at the end of the book, Henry "is never petulant, or impatient; for he remembers the real troubles that he was obliged silently to endure. He is always affectionate and obedient to his parents, for he recollects when no one gave him a kind word or look. He repays tenfold the love of his brother and sister, for he remembers the scoffing and unkindness, which he used to receive from the children of his different tormentors" (120-21).

Though we may rightly accuse Flint, on the basis of passages such as these, of again falling victim to the temptation of violating artistic decorum by too strong statement, and of making characters who are unbelievable in their motivations, yet generally considered such a character as Henry can be posited as necessary to the meaning of the parable that Flint relates. But, unfortunately, the character of Henry is not the real focus of the moral of the story. The moral of the story is a specifically providential one; not only does everything work out for the best, as it did, say, in *George Mason,* but Providence interferes directly in human affairs in order to teach humans a moral lesson. Hence, Flint has a pat explanation for the providential purpose which allowed Callendar and Tuttell to steal Henry. It is that Henry's parents had loved him too dearly, and "bitterly were [they] punished for this injudicious and unjust fondness."

To give Flint credit, he feels a bit uneasy about this conclusion: "I do not say, as some, who are good men notwithstanding, would say, that they were punished by heaven, for making their child an idol, and loving him more than their other children, and their God," he goes on. But mature reflection convinces him that there is more justice in this position than at first appears. "And yet I know not," he concludes, "when parents really allow their love for their children to run to a foolish and sinful excess, beyond what reason or religion authorise, why God may not justly punish such a fondness, by taking away the idol, to which their hearts are joined, and causing them to stand corrected, by leaving them nothing but himself to love" (16-17). As polemic theology this may be perfectly true; but as propaganda aimed at a juvenile audience it is woefully inept, and even the smallest child is likely to have some inkling of the fallacy in this philosophical position. For Henry himself hadn't done anything; indeed, he had been, from the beginning of the story, just the kind of little boy whom parents are supposed to find irresistible. From a child's point of view, the punishment Henry reaps seems rather out of proportion to what he has sown, and Flint's consolation at the end of the tale, that he "is improved by suffering" (120), is, from a youthful standpoint, likely to seem somewhat unconvincing.

V The Shoshonee Valley

If *George Mason* and *The Lost Child* are the nadir of Flint's fictional career, *The Shoshonee Valley* (1830) is, if not his best work, very near to it. This novel has always been critically neglected and is now unjustly forgotten. It represents Flint's final attempt to come to philosophical terms with the meaning of the advance of civilization, and in both profundity of conception and quality of execution it is, to my view at least, far superior to all Flint's other treatments of the theme. *The Shoshonee Valley* represents Flint's only extended foray into the romance country of the literary Indian—a republic dominated, though not exclusively occupied, by James Fenimore Cooper, to whom Flint is obviously indebted.[11] Though specific borrowings are unimportant, the general tone of the novel is unmistakably Cooper's. Flint seems to have at last arrived at some comprehension of what Cooper's moral tendency in fact is; when he describes the moral purpose of *The Shoshonee Valley*, for the only time in his fictional writing the term "moral" is not synonomous with "didactic." This passage is worth examination in detail:

This narrative contemplates [the Shoshonee Indians] at the point of the first palpable influence of the introduction of money, and what we call civilization. It cannot fail to present a spectacle of great moral interest. With an apparent accession of new ideas, new comforts, new wants, and new views of things present and to come, these simple people are always seen to forego their simplicity, and become less wise; to change their skins for dresses of cloth, and to begin to suffer from the inclemency of the seasons; and to learn the use of our medicines, and modes of applying them, and to become subject to new and more mortal diseases; in short, to melt away, through the influence of our boasted civilization, like the snow wreath of their hills, when a clear sun rises on their southern exposure (I, 25).

The rhetoric of this passage is pure Flint, but the philosophical implications are clearly Cooper's. The "spectacle of great moral interest," Flint tells us, is, in general terms, that of the irony of history. For the attempt to improve ends in demoralization; and civilization, at least for those being civilized, is tantamount to death. The passage implies—and the rest of *The Shoshonee Valley* makes good the implication—that the "moral interest" to be found in the story will come through contemplation of the action of the novel taken as a whole and not through an easy identification with some character whose actions and opinions are always "right." Hence the novel will not detail the conflict of "right" with "wrong" or of "good" with "evil" so much as it will explore the ironies inherent in the conflict between different conceptions of "good" and "right." This in turn implies a certain authorial sympathy not only with different viewpoints of "good" but, inversely, with a certain understanding of and compassion for the "evil" which the characters in the novel do and suffer.

The most startling specific change in Flint's fictional world involved in this different view of the nature of "morality" in literature is seen in the increased sympathy with which he treats the Shoshonee Indians. The passage quoted above suggests that the Indian view of the good life cannot be rejected out of hand, an opinion which Flint elsewhere totally denies; only in *The Shoshonee Valley* and its preliminary study, "Oolemba in Cincinnati," does he express approval of Indian ways.[12]

The principal source for *The Shoshonee Valley,* a short story entitled "Oolemba in Cincinnati," appeared in James Hall's *Western Souvenir* for 1829. It purports to be a story which Flint had heard at the campfire of a band of Indians who were moving west to escape the pressures of colonization. Flint and "an aged red man" (69) were the only strangers in this group, and the red man—Oolemba—told his story. Some five hundred moons ago, he said, he was a young man living in the virgin forest where Cincinnati now stands. He had had a son named Wansimmet; and, though he had heard rumors of the white men in Kentucky, had never actually seen any. When Wansimmet was seventeen, a few whites had come west, bringing whiskey on which the young man had gotten drunk. After recovering, Wansimmet, who realized whiskey was poison, had determined to fight the whites and had gone off to Kentucky to do so. He had returned west when the whites had become too strong, and soon afterwards "many huge and strange canoes" (74) had come down the Ohio, landed, and their white occupants had burned down Oolemba's cabin. Though Oolemba and Wansimmet had succeeded in wounding two whites, they realized the futility of struggle and went west, Wansimmet cursing the land as he left it.

On their Western trip Oolemba and Wansimmet had tried without success to unite the various Indian tribes against the whites. Eventually they had come to the Rocky Mountains and, after aimless wandering, had finally arrived in a valley where they had found "the Sho-sho-nee, a mild and good people" (84), who took them in. Wansimmet had become the first war chief of the Sho-sho-nee and had married Lenlennee, daughter of the first council chief. But a fierce Indian tribe from the West, supplied with guns by the whites, had raided the valley and killed almost all the Sho-sho-nee. Only Oolemba and a few Sho-sho-nee escaped; both Wansimmet and Lenlennee were killed. Oolemba had decided to return to Cincinnati, which he found so changed that he could not recognize it. After long searching, he had discovered the sycamore which had once sheltered his cabin, but the site itself was occupied by a bank. Realizing that there is now no place left for him in Cincinnati, Oolemba returns west to the remaining Sho-sho-nee. The story ends with a fairly conventional *ubi sunt*. Oolemba can only conclude:

"It is the will of the Great Spirit! The generations of leaves succeed each other on the trees! The waves follow each other, and break on the shore.—Men are as leaves and waves. The frost has come, and the red men are scattered to the winds! The pale-faces came after them! They too will give place to other generations."

The only course of action Oolemba can recommend is submission. The Indians must go west to get out of the white men's way. Flint's own reflection on the moral of the story is almost identical to Oolemba's: "I followed the hoary chief, in thought, on his long way to his desolate goal. I rose and started towards the regions of the rising sun, feeling as I went, that the days of man upon the earth, are as a shadow!" (100-1).

The conventional quality of the moral of this story must not cause us to overlook the way in which Oolemba's history is told. From his standpoint, the advent of the whites has brought nothing but tragedy; and, though he counsels submission, he does so only because he realizes the futility of resistance. Even in this paraphrase of the story, its resemblance to Cooper is clearly evident. Oolemba is a Delaware and, like Chingachgook, has seen a proud and mighty people dispersed before the oncoming whites. Wansimmet bears a strong resemblance to Uncas, and "Oolemba in Cincinnati" is in a way a short version of *The Last of the Mohicans*. But more important than the resemblance in specific details is the way in which the somber mood of "Oolemba" is created; like Cooper, Flint creates a pathetic effect by forcing the reader—himself one who has benefited from the progress of civilization—to identify with the victims of this progress; and thus he establishes an ambiguous and ironic view of history in the reader's own mind.

The "mild and good people" of the Sho-sho-nee to whom Oolemba returns become the central figures in *The Shoshonee Valley*. Though the Shoshonee are a definite historic Indian tribe, Flint obviously knows little about them. His Shoshonee are largely mental creations, and are not really flesh-and-blood Indians of a particular locality somewhere in the Rocky Mountains. In "Oolemba" the Sho-sho-nee had been described as "clearly the children of the pale-face" (84), and Flint elaborates this notion in *The Shoshonee Valley*. The Shoshonee "are a tall, finely formed, and comparatively fair haired race, more mild in manners, more polished and advanced in civilization, and more conversant with the arts of municipal life" than the neighboring Indians. "In fact, many of the females, unexposed by their condition to the sun and inclemencies of the seasons, are almost as fair, as the whites" (I, 7). Unlike their neighbors as well, they are basically an agricultural people with domestic animals which they have gotten from the Spanish settlements rather than a "savage" society of hunters. In short, they are not really Indians at all, at least as Flint knew Indians; rather they are a kind of metaphorical tribe, imbued with all the virtues of an agricultural (white) civilization, but unaffected by the vices—especially whiskey—of white society.[13] In his creation of the Shoshonee, Flint has made at least in part a civilization which contains the virtues of white society but not its defects, and part of his concern in telling the history of the Shoshonee is to demonstrate on an abstract and almost allegorical level the conflict of virtue with vice through the interaction of Shoshonee and white society.

The Shoshonee live "in a long and narrow vale of unparalleled wildness and beauty of scenery" (I, 7) which is surrounded by mountains covered with perpetual snow and through which runs a beautiful river, the Sewasserna. The valley is easy to cultivate, the soil is fertile, the valley is filled with game and exotic birds and the Sewasserna with delectable fish; the whole area is very much like the island on which Arthur Clenning lived—with the significant difference that to all the advantages of nature are added the blessings of society. The Shoshonee's existence is an almost Edenic one, but into any Eden may come a serpent; he comes into this one in the guise of the white race, who bring a poison apple "in the form of ardent spirits" (I, 17). The whites who invade the privacy of the Shoshonee are, as we expect from Flint, those dregs of society who have gone west to become frontiersmen. All of them "were, more or less, imbued with an instinctive fondness for the reckless savage life, alternately indolent and laborious, full and fasting, occupied in hunting, fighting, feasting, intriguing, and amours, interdicted by no laws, or difficult morals, or any restraints, but the invisible ones of Indian habit and opinion" (I, 21-22).

In addition to these occasional visitors, there are a number of more or less permanent white inhabitants among the Shoshonee. The most important of these is one William Weldon and his family. Weldon's reason for going west is by now familiar: he had been influenced to come to the valley by "the wild and pernicious sophism of Rousseau, that the savage is happier, than the social state" (I, 36-37). He had come with a Chinese wife named Yensi whom he had met in Canton when he had been a sailor. Weldon had brought no firewater, and "this circumstance raised him in the estimation of Ellswatta" (I, 49), the chief of the Shoshonee, who himself had married a foreigner, a Spanish girl named Josepha whom he had captured on a punitive raid against the Spanish settlements. Weldon and Yensi become fast friends of Ellswatta and Josepha. When both families have issue—Weldon, a daughter named Jessy; Ellswatta, a son named Areskoui—the implication is clear that the two races will ultimately be joined in marriage.

A more sinister white inhabitant of the valley is Trader Hatch, whose primary article of trade is whiskey and whose family motto, rendered into English, runs "money is the main chance" (I, 60). He takes an Indian wife, and at the wedding ceremonies gets all his Indian guests drunk on his whiskey. Indeed, Hatch's rising popularity among the Indians is due almost entirely to his freedom with whiskey, and his presence is of grave concern to Ellswatta. Later, two other whites come to the valley; Elder Wood, a Baptist minister from Kentucky, and Baptiste Dettier, a Canadian *coureur du bois*. The Indians respect Elder Wood, though he has little success in converting them to Christianity nor, more important to the symbolic structure of the novel, in winning them from Trader Hatch's whiskey. While Elder Wood becomes a staunch friend of Ellswatta and Weldon and eventually goes to live in Weldon's home, Baptiste soon becomes an associate of Trader Hatch, as does later Nelesho, the young chief of the Shienne, a tribe of Indians whom the Shoshonee have defeated in war and who live with them in the valley in a state of uneasy peace.

The significance of the various white inhabitants of the valley should now be clear in terms of a larger symbolic context. For one preoccupation of *The Shoshonee Valley* is an examination of the nature of government, and this examination is prosecuted through the metaphorical discussion of "good counsel"—represented by Ellswatta, Weldon, and Elder Wood, and their appeal to law, reason, and religion—and of "evil counsel"—

represented by Trader Hatch and his party, who appeal to passion. In this context the rather priggish division of men into virtuous and vicious on the basis of those who drink and those who don't makes good symbolic sense; for Trader Hatch's use of whiskey becomes a metaphor of the demagogue's appeal to the passions rather than to the reason of his partisans. Flint's sad commentary on government, to anticipate for a moment, is that the appeal to passion is ultimately the stronger. The point is made more specific by Yensi, who realizes that, in a society such as the Shoshonee where there is no law but the force of custom, passion must inevitably be stronger than reason; for the appeal to vice is more immediately compelling than that to virtue. Yensi pleads again and again with her husband and with Elder Wood, "who alike maintained the wild sophism of Rousseau, in regard to the superiority of savage over social life," to return to civilization, "where they might spend their days in the security of law and order" (I, 80). But she is unheeded.

As the years go by, the uneasy equilibrium of the valley becomes even more precarious; the Shoshonee rally around Ellswatta and his son Areskoui, who is elected, when eighteen years old, first war chief. The disaffected Shienne look to Nelesho (and, parenthetically, to Trader Hatch's whiskey) to redress their grievances against the conquering Shoshonee. The situation worsens when two young men, Julius Landino and Frederic Belden, whose ship has landed at Astoria, come up the Sewasserna to see the Shoshonee. They predictably woo Jessy, who is at first smitten with both of them—significantly enough— because they remind her of the heroes in her father's romances. They also win her attention by accounts of the "great world" outside the valley, much to the unhappiness of Areskoui, whose unaffected love for Jessy meets with no return. The showiness of the strangers and their immediate popular success with Jessy emphasize again the major theme of the novel. For Trader Hatch and his whiskey are "popular" with the Indians too; conversely, Ellswatta, Elder Wood, and William Weldon are not.

Jessy, however, eventually begins to discover that the smooth exteriors of the two strangers do not accurately express their inner characters. For, though Julius is a genuine debauchee, Frederic (in a manner typical of Flint's heroes) is only young, romantic, and immature. He soon realizes that Julius does not wish only to engage in a harmless flirtation, and he joins forces with Areskoui to preserve Jessy from him. Julius becomes an intimate of Nelesho, Trader Hatch, and the disaffected Shienne, and engineers the kidnaping of Jessy, who is taken away to an inaccessible spot in the mountains. Julius appears and attempts to seduce her, but an old Indian crone named Maniteewah helps her to escape a fate worse than death by means of a well-worn ruse. Julius had placed a sleeping potion in Jessy's wine, and Jessy, warned of this by Maniteewah, switches wine glasses. The utter conventionality of this abduction and attempted seduction may cause us to miss its thematic importance. For Maniteewah and Julius are complete opposites: he is a whited sepulchre; she, though physically repulsive, is morally above reproach. The point of the episode is clear; Jessy has been taught that appearances can be deceiving and that the garb of a romantic hero is not an invariable sign of moral virtue. She is finally rescued by a party led by Areskoui, and Julius is deported to Astoria.

The thematic implications of *The Shoshonee Valley* are by now clear. Ultimately Flint is ringing changes on the theme of the ambiguity of appearances. All the characters in the novel have finally to realize that apparent good is not necessarily ultimate good. On one level this realization is shown in the "political" plot of the novel, where the apparent "good" represented by Trader Hatch and his whiskey is a real evil, but the Shoshonee are unable to understand this. The same theme is at the basis of the "love" plot, where Jessy is educated to recognize the real evil which lies behind the superficial goodness of Julius, and conversely, the real goodness in the unassuming character of Areskoui. William Weldon and Elder Wood are also victims of illusion, specifically of the sophism of Rousseau that the savage state is superior to the social. This "sophism," in terms of the parable of *The Shoshonee Valley*, is the philosophical metaphor which supports the entire book. Put in general terms, it shows an unwillingness to face the facts of the world as it is, and to imply onto a certain state of society a purely imaginary moral value which it does not in reality contain.

The plot of the second volume of *The Shoshonee Valley* is easily told. Trader Hatch and Nelesho become more successful in converting the Shienne to drunkenness and anarchy; Hatch succeeds in rousing a bunch of drunken Shienne to attack Weldon's home; and Weldon and Yensi are killed in a final metaphorical refutation of the notion that the savage state is superior to the social. In the general battle which follows, Areskoui kills Nelesho, and the Shoshonee massacre the drunken Shienne. Jessy—on whom her dead mother's point about the precariousness of life in a society where there are no laws has not been lost—decides to leave the Shoshonee and goes, with Elder Wood as her protector, to Astoria. There she is spirited away by Julius and is carried off to "the isle of Ostroklotz, two hundred leagues north of the Oregon" (II, 96), where she is again rescued in the nick of time from death or worse by Elder Wood, Areskoui, Frederic, and the loyal Shoshonee. This time Julius is not banished but put to death by the Shoshonee.

But all is not to end happily. When the rescue party returns to the valley, Areskoui asks Jessy to marry him, but she refuses since she wishes no longer to live in the precariousness of the savage state. She tries to influence him to marry Katrina, her servant who is in love with him; but Areskoui is not to be swayed. With stoical Indian reserve he takes Jessy and Elder Wood to a cliff high above a lake in the middle of the valley which she had always loved. He bids them look at the lake:

> "Father [he says to Elder Wood], seest thou this still evening and yonder fair valley? Is it not, as if the Master of Life had come upon the scene, bringing joy and peace? How beautiful are the clouds in the sky? and how quiet is every thing but this beating breast? But yonder, in the depths of the blue lake, is a world still more beautiful. There are the green trees, the mountains, the scaling eagle, the skimming swallow; and there, too, is Wakona [the Indian name for Jessy]—still brighter than here. How beautiful! Thither flies away to remain in shadow all that is pleasant above. There on those hills the spirit, which has here been imprisoned, can soar again, and look at the sun, which has left us behind the hills. The spirit of Areskoui longs to become, as yonder eagle" (II, 221).

In context the passage is marvelously effective. Areskoui is proclaiming his longing for the ideal world, one where pain is unknown and where everything is more beautiful than in the complex and tragic one of everyday. But the metaphorical drift of the passage makes the reader suspect that this ideal world is something more than an ingenious philosophical construct of Areskoui's; it is only to be found in death. And, after proclaiming the power of the ideal, Areskoui leaps from the cliff to his death in the beautiful world he discerns in the water.

The remaining whites leave the Shoshonee Valley and take ship at Astoria. Though Jessy promises to marry Frederic, her inheritance from her father of a "romantic" world view has made it impossible for her to live in the real world symbolized by the Shoshonee Valley. She too yearns for the ideal, where the complexities and tragedy of life are resolved in beauty; and one day she slips over the side of the ship to join Areskoui in the splendor of the world she sees mirrored in the water.

The Shoshonee Valley suffers much in paraphrase. Like the Leatherstocking Tales, its esthetic effect depends greatly on mood, and mood evaporates quickly from a plot summary. Flint's ultimate purpose in *The Shoshonee Valley* is to examine the pathos inherent in the conflict between two parts of man's nature—his longing for perfection and his necessity to compromise. All the characters in the novel face this problem: all must come to terms with the sad fact that the ideal world is unattainable. William Weldon dies because of his assumption that perfection may be found in an earthly paradise; Areskoui and Jessy kill themselves because they cannot live in a real world which does not conform to an ideal one they had desperately wished for. At the end of the novel we have only Frederic and Elder Wood left, both truly wayfaring strangers. Our last sight of them is on a ship at sea, in mourning, traveling from a desolate past to an uncertain future. Like Flint's earlier novels, *The Shoshonee Valley* is a book about education, but where the implied motto of his earlier books had been "Ye shall know the truth, and the truth shall make you free," that of *The Shoshonee Valley* is rather "For in much wisdom is much grief: and he that increaseth knowledge increaseth sorrow."

CHAPTER **5**

Man of Letters

THOUGH FLINT'S MOST EXTENSIVE—and probably his most important—literary work was done as a geographer-historian and as a novelist-moralist, a balanced assessment of his career must take into account those miscellaneous writings which do not fit into these categories. Flint, always interested in the world around him, was always ready with vehement, if occasionally none too profound, opinions about it. These opinions, though some of them seem sadly dated to us today, were in his own time listened to with respect. A laudatory review of his career remarked with approval that "his works are not merely to amuse," and went on to praise him specifically on the grounds that "more than any other writer of his country he has labored to instruct, to inform, and to impart knowledge where knowledge was required, and difficult of attainment." Indeed, to this reviewer Flint was "almost as versatile an author as Goldsmith."[1] Neither Flint nor his audience would have understood the modern notion that, in order to speak with authority about something esoteric and involved, the knowledge of a specialist was required. This idea would have smacked of the superstition of the Dark Ages, rather than the clear reason of the Enlightenment. For man was capable of understanding with only a little application: Nature and God both stood revealed in the simple light of reason.

Though this idea seems painfully simple-minded to us today, we must remember that Flint and his readers did not ask the same questions of phenomena which we ask, and that, as a result, the answers they found were not so silly as they seem to us. As the quotation would suggest, Flint and his readers asked moral questions of phenomena rather than questions of obscure matters of fact. Flint's purpose in almost all his writing is moral, and the knowledge he imparts is not that of the laboratory or of the medical school, but that of the philosopher's study.

I *The Handmaid of Theology*

One of Flint's major lifelong interests was science. Early in his life a laboratory had been one of the causes of friction between him and his parishioners, and his interest in science continued to his death. As a geographer, no more need be said of him here; but as a laboratory scientist, some additional comments may be in order.

Flint's most ambitious scientific work was the *Lectures Upon Natural History* (1833). This book, which was received with almost unanimous critical disapproval, is an attempt to present in popularized form "enough of the philosophy and general principles of science, to furnish materials for thought and conversation upon the subjects discussed" (vii). The subjects discussed are legion: "The Natural Laws," "Botany. Botanical Sensation," "Insects," "Starry Heavens. Rivers. Animal Harmonies," "Electricity," "Weight of the Atmosphere," "Birds," "Winds," "Air," "Carbonic Acid Gas," "Geology. The Age of the World," "Political Economy," and "Vaccination" are only some of the first chapters of the book. The philosophy and general principles which they illustrate, however, are not quite what a modern scientific investigator would anticipate. They are, as the last lectures of the book remind us, "Choice of Pursuit," "Decision of Character," "The Proper Selection of Books," "The Place and Ritual of Worship," and "What Are the Best Evidences of True Wisdom in Character?" The answer to the question posed by the title of this last lecture reveals the point of the book: man should understand the "certain, invariable, irresistible laws" of God (398) and mold himself to be in harmony with them. The book, in sum, is not really a scientific text at all, but an expanded proof of the existence of God, based primarily on the argument from design. The purpose of the *Lectures* had been explicitly stated in the first lecture on "The Natural Laws": "Every new fact in the study of nature, when rightly interpreted, becomes a new evidence of the intelligence and benevolence of a first cause" (14).

The most immediately apparent weakness in the *Lectures* is that the facts in the study of nature which Flint discovers are often rather hard to believe. The "gray-squirrel," for instance, which "in crossing our wide rivers, selects a piece of bark on the shore, of a form favourable for sailing, on which it embarks, erecting its tufted tail for a sail, which it veers with admirable precision to the wind" (73), is likely to seem to the skeptical reader a creature more of romance than history, even though Flint's explanation of the purpose of his bushy tail does relieve Providence from the imputation of having created something useless. Likewise we have this account of an experiment: "a long black hair from a horse's mane was left in a wooden trough, to soak in rain water, during the sultry days of August, for ten or twelve days. At the end of that time it had become white, and had acquired a protuberance at one extremity, like a head. It moved about, folded, and unfolded itself, showed sensibility when touched, and had become in fact that singular animal, of which naturalists, as far as I know, have taken no notice; but which farmers know well by the name hair-snake" (49). This statement called forth the almost unanimous derision of the reviewers, even though Flint claimed to have performed the experiment himself.

Such carelessness with data is to be expected in a scientific investigation conducted for purposes such as Flint's; for, if the purpose of research is to discover general principles which lead us to knowledge of a first cause, one general principle is as good as another. The study of phenomena soon becomes redundant, and errors in fact become of little importance once the principles have been demonstrated. But more serious than Flint's errors of fact are errors in theory; like that of *The Lost Child*, the moral of the *Lectures* does not always quite fit the facts.

Most thinkers arguing from design have been more cautious than Flint in attributing specific beneficent purpose to the affairs of creation. If, in Paley's example, the first cause stands in rela-tion to its effects as a watchmaker to his watch, once the watch has been made the watchmaker leaves it alone. Flint is not satisfied with this rather distant and impersonal first cause. For the world does not only run, he thinks, according to im-mutable laws, but these laws are universally beneficent. The world does not only exist, but it exists for some good reason;

the universal laws are particularly beneficent as well as universal. "The ultimate tendency" of the world "is, to cause it to become a more convenient and happy abode for its sentient inhabitants of every description" (274). If this statement is so, how does one explain evil? A number of possibilities are open. First, it might be possible to show that evil is becoming less powerful in the world: This is self-evident, Flint says, when we consider that man's increased knowledge of universal (scientific) laws has enabled him to improve his physical well-being. Second, it is possible that apparent evil is really good: This may be shown, Flint says, by considering volcanoes, which in some mysterious way purify the ocean, or by considering poisons, which some-how—he is vague on just exactly how—purify the atmosphere. However fatuous these examples may seem, the principles upon which they depend may at least be convincingly argued. But Flint is not content with arguing the general principles; the world is not only generally benevolent, but particularly as well. And here his optimism runs into some apparent opposition from those very facts whose beneficence he has so blithely postulated.

Consider, for example, the steam engine, his prime example of applied scientific principle working for human good. The steam engine has enabled mankind to build boats which can ascend the Mississippi; yet "unhappily, either avarice, or rashness, or intoxication, or puerile and reckless ambition to make a quick trip, or the uses of imperfect or worn out boilers, or all in conjunction, have produced many fatal explosions, by which hundreds of lives have been lost; and associations of terror, connected with travelling by steam have tended to diminish the number of passengers, and the sense of security in those, who still continue to travel in this way" (312). It is perfectly true that none of this danger is the fault of steam in itself, and Flint could easily conclude his point, as Aquinas would, by distinguishing between accidents, which may be apparent evils, and ends, which must be good. Yet he does not do so, and, though the passage ends on a note of vague worry, Flint is ultimately unable to fit the beneficence of steam and the disaster of explosion into any kind of philosophical whole.

The point is even clearer in an interesting passage which concludes a discussion of the formation of snow and ice. Flint describes how, in the winter, snow and ice form upon the tops of mountains and then, in the spring, melt into streams which nourish the pleasant meadows beneath. The beginning of the passage gives a pat example of the argument from design, yet the rather odd conclusion is worth quoting at length:

> From the height of a cliff, you contemplate one of the deep valleys among the Alps. The cattle are seen ruminating in their pastures, and the smokes stream aloft from the peaceful domestic hearths. You behold heaped above you, hills upon hills, the accumulated snows and ices of ages glittering in mid air in the sun-beams. Overcharged by their own weight, or undermined by a new-formed mountain-torrent, a fearful noise, announcing in advance the doom of the vale below, gives warning that an avalanche has broken from its deep foundations. The villagers in the fields have only time to fly to the embrace of their wives and children before all is whelmed in the common destruction! The fair valley, lately the abode of peace and love, is buried a hundred fathoms deep with snows and rocks and ruins (241).

In terms of the argument from design, such a passage seems to require some explanation. Here, the very laws which on the one hand beneficently provide the valley with water, on the other destroy it. There is no question—as in the discussion of the steam engine—of human meddling with the divine plan. As it stands, the description of the avalanche is a complete metaphorical refutation of the premise of the *Lectures;* yet Flint is totally unconscious of this. The passage ends with this description; Flint feels no need to explain this apparent refutation of universal good will.

Just as Flint's geographies show him at his best as a scientist, the *Lectures* show him at his worst. In the collection of fact— the above examples of the squirrel and the hair-snake notwithstanding—he is generally acute. He believes in the primary importance of observation in determining scientific truth and, as a geographer at least, is impatient with second-hand reporting and with wild stories. Yet his attempts to fit scientific facts into some kind of larger truth are always disastrous, chiefly because his explanation is invariably too simplistic to fit them. Like all teleologists, Flint begins with a general principle and from it deduces the facts which go to prove it. This method of course is the complete opposite of the scientific one. The

Lectures in one way bear a remarkable resemblance to Flint's worst novel, *The Lost Child.* In both works Flint begins with facts—scientific or historical—which are to be interpreted, and ends with an explanation which does not fit them.

II *Literary Criticism*

Like his scientific writing, Flint's literary criticism is a mixture of particular observations and general theories. His theoretical criticism is generally polemical and, as one would expect on the basis of his own literary practice, is highly moral in emphasis. Literature is a didactic art, he thinks; and, when it is not didactic, it ceases to be literature. Surprisingly, however, very little of Flint's criticism deals with the purpose of literature, nor does much of it attempt to appraise the merits of specific works of art. Neither does Flint often attempt a general theory of literary criticism. His constant critical concern is rather to explain the social obstacles which face the writer—particularly the American writer—and his criticism is always tendentious. The obstacles the writer faces are always at least partially moral ones as well as economic or historical facts of life. His most extended analysis of American literature in the *Western Monthly Review* is significantly titled "Impediments of American Literature," and his later discussion in the *Knickerbocker* bears a similar title, "Obstacles to American Literature." In his most expanded work of literary criticism, a series of eleven articles for the London *Athenaeum,* most of his emphasis is again on the difficulties facing the writer—specifically, though not exclusively, the American one.

The difficulties, impediments, and obstacles which the (American) writer faces ultimately reduce themselves to the unwillingness of the (American) public to accept literature as a serious pursuit. The man of letters in America is, Flint says in what seems a peculiarly modern point of view, "regarded with a sort of humiliating pity."[2] American society militates against him in a number of ways. In the *Knickerbocker* discussion of "Obstacles to American Literature," Flint makes his most schematic and logical statement about the problems which separate the American writer from a successful career. He begins this article by posing the question of why, with all the literary effort in America, there is no national literature. He notices the lack, not so much of poets who contribute occasional verse to magazines (such as the *Knickerbocker*), as of a professional class of men of letters. There are many American literary amateurs, Flint says, but very few professionals. The vocation of "letters" is not a popular one.

Flint distinguishes seven reasons for this. First, he says, the practice of letters has no prestige value in America. Since, as he goes on to remark, it is also an ill-paid vocation, no men of talent take it up. There are no rewards in either prestige or money to be found in the practice of literature, and as a result men of ambition shun it. Flint suggests that the government should encourage letters, with money if necessary, in order to make the vocation more highly prized. Second, and closely allied to the first, is the lack of a literary metropolis where men of letters might meet and exchange views. The rivalry which exists between the various American cities does a disservice to letters, in Flint's view, because it fosters a spirit in which each uncritically "boosts" its own writers, irrespective of their merits. What Flint wishes to exist in America is a literary metropolis such as London where men of letters might gather and live, or, since such a metropolis obviously must grow of itself rather than being planned in advance, a society such as the French Academy with quasi-official status in questions of literary taste. In an earlier article Flint had suggested that such an academy might gather each year in Philadelphia to pass judgment on the quality of recently published books.[3]

Third, Flint remarks the absolute necessity for American literary emancipation from Great Britain. He mentions specifically the injury to American writers which arises from the fact that there is no international copyright agreement with Britain. The lack of such a copyright means that works of English authors can be pirated and printed cheaply in America without payment of royalty. As a result, American books cannot compete on the open market with English editions. Flint also sees that this lack of copyright agreement militates against not only Americans but authors generally; for it enables publishers to print their works without, quite often, giving them any monetary compensation at all. But American literary dependence on Britain has more important consequences than the merely pragmatic ones of lack of copyright protection for American authors. If Americans are slavish adorers of only English models, American literature can never amount to anything. American dependence upon English models, Flint perceptively argues, is fostered to a great degree by the reviews: they exalt English literary productions and imply, when they do not openly state, the inferiority of the American. In another context he points out that—all strident American political anglophobia to the contrary—"there is still a deep and innate preference of an English book, as such, over an American one on the same subject and with the same pretensions. Deny this, as many pretend to do; it is manifest that to have been produced in the parent country, and to have come over the sea to us, gives it a value which it would not have received, as a native production.[4] American dependence on England is not an isolated phenomenon; rather it is emblematic of a certain American unwillingness to accept something unknown "as such" over a better-known model, with superior credentials:

> Speak of a fine writer of our own country, and near home, and you instantly hear about Mr. Jeffrey, and Dr. Chalmers, and Mr. Brougham, and Sir Walter Scott; and in such a way, as if they had left all hope of competition at an immeasurable distance behind them. . . . This general and slavish notion . . . should be banished; and we ought to be impressed, that if we will look as intently, and study as patiently, and feel as deeply, we shall write as well in America, as in Europe.[5]

This attitude of uncritical admiration of "respectable" models is more universal than a slavish homage to England. On a local level Americans betray the same habit of mind. "A western writer," Flint mentions in an article in the *Western Monthly Review*, "we are sorry to say, finds more favor any where else, than in the West. No where are they [the inhabitants of America] so slavishly determined, that a prophet shall find little honor in his own country."[6] In other words, there is a kind of pecking order of snobbish preference: quote Cooper or Irving or Longfellow, and a Bostonian will quote Scott or Goldsmith or Byron; quote Hall or Flint or Bryan, and a Cincinnatian will quote Cooper or Irving or Longfellow.

Flint's fourth reason seems to the modern reader the most

perceptive. He flatly says that letters are not prized in America because "the spirit of the age and country is opposed to the progress of literature" (II, 164). He specifically calls attention to the American fascination with what he calls the "physical"— the twentieth century would use the term "material"—aspects of life, an attitude which militates against the practice of letters. He mentions the commercial nature of American society, and he remarks generally the growth of materialism in the modern world. This materialism poses, he says, a long-run problem for the man of letters. Literature does not pay for itself, and probably never did. Consequently it requires some kind of support from those who are interested in it. Yet contrary to American belief, literature, whether it pays for itself or not, is an absolute social necessity: "A certain number of *littérateurs* is as much called for, in every well ordered community, to elevate thought, inspire intellectuality, and lift up the attention from mere physical aims, to aspirations of a moral and internal nature, as the class of operatives,"[7] he elsewhere remarks. Yet the benefits of a class of *littérateurs* are not immediately apparent to those whose interests are "physical"; as a result, men of letters are neglected by those who could afford to support them, and literature languishes. Even in Britain, Flint mentions, this preoccupation with the "physical" is becoming increasingly important; even there the commercial spirit militates against letters. Men of true taste, therefore, who in an aristocratic society patronized literature, are becoming increasingly rare; and those who could either play the role of Maecenas themselves or influence the government to play it for them are becoming at once fewer in numbers and less powerful.[8] Those who can afford to play Maecenas are precisely those whose interest in the "physical" keeps them from doing so.

Flint's fifth reason is the presence in America of too many writers of inferior ability. "Literature seems likely to perish under a deluge of its own exuberance" (II, 164). This point seems to be, at first glance, inconsistent with the overall tendency of Flint's other view that literature is dying on the vine, but in the context of his sixth reason it becomes clearer. This sixth reason is a reference to the American habit of "puffing"—of giving indiscriminate praise to a book in order to sell it. Here Flint is remarking the advertising spirit of America, the ideal of the "promoter," who, like the "booster" of a particular city whom he had mentioned earlier, is interested only in selling something, and to whom the quality of the merchandise is a matter of supreme indifference. Because of this habit of "puffing," Flint acutely perceives, the prospective reader requires some kind of objective appraisal of works of literature in order to aid him in his selection of books. Few people who are not professional men of letters have the time to read most of the books which appear, and hence the average man requires some guidance in his purchase of reading matter. Given the lack of a society similar to the French Academy which might utter *ex cathedra* pronouncements about the relative value of various recently published books, the only authoritative source to which the prospective reader can turn is the reviews. But the reviews have shirked their responsibility as judges of letters, and Flint's strictures on their shilly-shallying are his most perceptive and convincing negative argument against them. The reviews operate "on the safe non-committal principle" of playing safe, and "generally find in the books reviewed no more than a text for an abstract discussion, a thousand leagues from any analysis or review of the book, that shall enable the purchaser to determine whether to possess himself of it or not. . . . We are well aware, that they contain many sensible and eloquent articles; but we could wish, that they were more direct, laconic, downright, fearless, and just; and especially that all reviews were, what they purport to be, analyses and fair awards of the high court of literature of the books reviewed" (II, 167).

Flint's final objection—what he calls the "most formidable impediment to American literature" (II, 167)—is the political interest of the mass of Americans. In a country where "the most stupid private citizen becomes an oracle, as soon as he is elected a member of congress" (II, 168), it is more than ordinarily difficult to tell false prophets from true. This objection comes down to Flint's opinion that American interest in politics is not philosophical and profound, but sensational and trivial. Americans are fascinated not by the meaning of the political process, but by the unimportant details of government. American political interest is another aspect of that spirit of the age which Flint had remarked in his fourth reason as being hostile to literature. Americans are too much involved in the specific to pay attention to the universal; their interests are too pragmatic, too material, and too deeply based in the here and now for literature to be much prized among them. They lack time for reflection, nor have they much interest in meditation.

When all these obstacles to literature are taken into account, however, Flint's final prognosis for the future of letters is not a gloomy one. Though it is true that the present "is pre-eminently an age of gross and absorbing avarice," in which "the estimated value of every thing is just what it will bring in money," and where "love, matrimony, religion, all is a matter of speculation, reduced to the simplicity of the decimal scale of dollars and eagles" (II, 164), there is no reason why the future should be this way. The very avarice and lust for gain which make the present so difficult a time for the practice of letters will inevitably bring about a future period of prosperity where things of the mind will be more highly prized. Materialism, Flint sees, is ultimately a means to the end of removing man from the necessity of caring for the material; in the future, more men than ever in the history of the world will be removed from want and from the necessity for toil, and will be free to devote themselves to interests which are not immediately practical. When that time comes, "men will ... better understand, and more implicitly respect, the moral and organic laws of the universe." In this "golden age," as Flint refers to it, "education will be conducted towards a specific and definite end. Those natural and moral faculties only will be developed, which subserve the end of our being."[9] When the "means" of life will take care of themselves, man may concern himself with its "end." At that time literature will be prized and the man of letters honored.

III *Paraphrases*

It is not surprising that a man who felt as strongly as Flint that one of the purposes of literature was the dissemination of information should have devoted much of his literary endeavor to making available useful knowledge which he himself had not discovered. Great portions of his various histories and geographies are paraphrases of the work of other investigators, and much of the material in the *Western Monthly Review* is similarly derivative. Even the *Lectures Upon Natural History* is in part

a paraphrase of Aimé Martin's *Lettres à Sophie* (Paris, 1825),
though Flint has much changed it in both form and example.
More ambitious than these are two full-length free translations
which Flint made in his later years. These are, respectively, a
paraphrase of Francis Xavier Joseph Droz's *Sur L'Art D'Être
Heureux* which Flint published as *The Art of Being Happy*
(1832), and a novel, the original of which I have not been
able to identify, which Flint acknowledges only as coming
"from the French" and which he entitles *The Bachelor Reclaimed
or Celibacy Vanquished* (1834).

The Art of Being Happy is told in a series of twenty-six letters
based on, though not identical with, Droz's original text. In
addition Flint adds a series of voluminous notes to the end
of the volume in which he explicates those parts of the argument
to which he thinks his readers might object, and where he also
calls attention to selections in the body of the work which he
finds particularly perceptive. His translation, he says in the
"Advertisement" which precedes the text of the book, does not
pretend to be literal. For one thing, Droz writes a strongly
idiomatic French which is "laconic sometimes to the point of
obscurity" and which is filled with local references which Flint
has either eliminated or changed. But his translation, he says,
is true to the spirit of the work, if not to the letter; and "the
general bearing of the work" is "the inculcation . . . of the truth
that *virtue is happiness*" (iii-iv).

The moral purpose of the work and the ultimate conclusions
drawn about how man may in fact be happy bear a close
resemblance to Flint's later remarks in the *Lectures Upon
Natural History*. "Religion and philosophy"—as, in the later work,
religion and science—"will be found resting on the same immutable foundation," and true philosophy "finds the Creator everywhere, and always acting in wisdom and power" (9-10). Happiness consists in the discovery of the immutable laws of the
universe and, once discovered, in conformity to them. Thus
happiness is only to be found in the limiting of our desires to
what the immutable laws of nature will permit us to achieve,
and the watchword of Droz—and Flint—is finally "moderation."
Dependent on the idea that we must limit our desires to what
we may reasonably expect to attain is the notion that true
happiness may best be found within oneself, in an environment

over which one has more or less complete control. The cultivation of the pleasures of the mind becomes the surest road to happiness, and the pleasures of art become the most real pleasures. The "indulgence of the imagination," Flint says in his notes, is ultimately the application of reason to a nonexistent world. The pleasure we find in art is in the last analysis a rational contemplation of a world better than the everyday world, a world "peopled with nobler beings, acting from higher motives, and showing a happier existence" than the world we see around us. In Flint's arresting phrase, we find pleasure in literature because it succeeds "in substituting the beautiful possible from [for] the tame real." And, Flint concludes, "if we find innocent happiness in this celestial castle-building, are we not employing reason, only in a different direction from the common?" (269).

Though this passage sounds as if Flint suggests that the value of art lies in its ability to give us an escape from reality, his point is really more profound. By contemplating "the beautiful possible" we may penetrate through the phenomena of life to the "immutable foundation" on which life is built. Art is not an escape from life but a means of interpreting it. We can now see why Flint finds Droz's argument so compelling. For, if the end of life is happiness and if happiness consists of understanding the immutable laws upon which life depends, art may help us to understand life by presenting a parable of it by means of which our minds may penetrate through the flux of experience.

The Bachelor Reclaimed is a much less profound work than *The Art of Being Happy*, and it is difficult to explain the laudatory review given it by the *Knickerbocker*—which stated that "Mr. Flint has performed a most acceptable service, in presenting the American reader with a good translation of this interesting work"[10]—on any grounds other than the fact that Flint had recently been editor of that periodical. Flint's own reason for translating the novel, he tells us in the Preface, is that its "interest is not made to depend upon one or many fine passages, but a uniform convergence of every incident and the whole tenor of the book towards a single result—the triumph of love over the most inveterate and rooted prejudices" (v). This is, he goes on to say, "a useful moral" (the reviewer for the

Knickerbocker is more emphatic; he says "the moral is capital") and one which is basic to most of Flint's own fiction. In *Francis Berrian, Arthur Clenning, George Mason,* and a number of his shorter works, happiness is ultimately found with wife and family; and *The Bachelor Reclaimed* single-mindedly makes this point explicit again. It details the reclamation of one Lord Milford from the fate of bachelorhood. While on a Continental tour, Lord Milford meets the sixty-year-old Marquis d'Azemar and his beautiful sixteen-year-old wife Adrienne. He falls in love with Adrienne, though of course he cannot marry her. Soon Providence, in the form of the French Revolution, intervenes; the Marquis dies; and Adrienne eventually comes under the protection of Lord Milford—who is now Lord Moreland, since he has succeeded to a title and to an immense property. After numerous melodramatic adventures, Lord Moreland finally realizes that he can only be happy if married to Adrienne. Accordingly he marries her; and, in a scene supposedly fraught with symbolic significance, he resigns from the Bachelor's Club which he had founded.

Had this story been told with any humor it might not have been so silly; for, though the moral may be unexceptionable, the tale is tedious in the extreme. Yet Flint thought so much of it that he attempted another paraphrase of it for the *Knickerbocker*. "A Chapter in the Life of a Bachelor, A South American Story," appeared in the January, 1834, issue. Though the title suggests that Flint had again turned to his earlier theme of South American romance, the story is actually only *The Bachelor Reclaimed* turned out in new finery. Lord Moreland is now called Henry Fellowes Selwyn; Adrienne is Marcia Aurelia; and the Marquis d'Azemar is now the Conde Stefano Agramente. The scene of the story has been changed from France and England to Cuba and Mexico, and Selwyn owns a Cuban coffee plantation where Lord Moreland had been a landed aristocrat. The plot of the short story exactly follows that of the novel up to the point where Selwyn-Moreland meets Agramente-d'Azemar, where it breaks off. The implication is clear that subsequent issues of the *Knickerbocker* would contain more of the history of Henry Fellowes Selwyn, but no future installments actually appeared in it. The reason for Flint's decision to drop the story must remain conjectural; the most likely explanation is that ill health forced him to resign all ambitious literary projects. *The Bachelor Reclaimed* was his last book-length work; after it appeared, he wrote only two other short stories before his death.

Flint's failure to complete the history of Henry Fellowes Selwyn is not a major loss to American letters. In his treatment of the theme of the reclaimed bachelor Flint has fallen prey to the familiar weakness which always more or less mars his fiction—didacticism. *The Bachelor Reclaimed* is much more like *The Lost Child* than it is like *The Shoshonee Valley*. The reader is never allowed to forget for one moment the didactic purpose of the story; and, though the characters of the work are nobler beings than those we see around us, they are also infinitely duller. Flint himself was "inclined to believe" that *The Bachelor Reclaimed*, like *The Lost Child*, was "based upon real incidents," and that substantially the story was "a true story of the French revolution."[11] This may be so, though most readers would probably be inclined to doubt it; but, even if it is true, the real moral of *The Bachelor Reclaimed*, like that of *The Lost Child*, is that biography—real or imagined—is not the same as art.

IV *Later Fiction*

When Flint left Cincinnati for the East in 1833, his fictional career was almost over. Most of his later writing appears in the *Knickerbocker*, of which he was editor for a short time and with which he was associated until his death. Ironically, his best later short story was the only one not written specifically for the *Knickerbocker*. An ambitious tale supposedly based on Flint's own experience, it appeared as "The Blind Grandfather" in *The Token and Atlantic Souvenir* at the end of 1833.

"The Blind Grandfather" is, on the surface, a "shocker." Flint tells how the boat on which he had been a passenger had run into a headwind on Lake Erie and had put ashore for the night in the hope that the wind would change by morning. He had gone to a cabin to entreat lodging and had met a blind man—the grandfather of the story—and his granddaughter, fifteen-year-old Ruth. During the evening the grandfather tells Flint the story of his life. He had emigrated west with his wife and, after an inauspicious beginning, had managed to make a comfortable living. He and his wife had been happy, and a daughter named Ruth had been born to them. His wife, who had been "excessively alarmed at thunder" (257), had once said to him: "I have a presentiment that I shall die by lightning" (258). Sure enough, a thunderstorm blew up; she was killed and he blinded by a lightning bolt. He had compensated for his loss of vision by building a better world in his mind's eye—an action which Flint had approved in another context—but he had also turned his love too much toward his daughter Ruth. Like the father of *The Lost Child,* his daughter was, he says, "the single magnet of all my heart's earthly affections," and he "loved her to the excess of a sinful idolatry" (261). When Ruth grew up, she was seduced by a land speculator and had a child by him. (The irony here is wonderful; the grandfather, contemplating the beautiful world which exists only in his mind's eye, cannot "see" what is happening.) The grandfather christened the child Ruth for her mother who soon after died, leaving him and his infant granddaughter to live alone together in their cabin. At this point the story ends with the grandfather's final remark to his now almost grown granddaughter: "I beseech thee, Ruth, restrain thy tears, God survives, although thy aged grandfather, must shortly go down to the dust. Some one will be found to protect thee. Doubt it not" (264).

"The Blind Grandfather" is easily Flint's best short story. With the longer *Shoshonee Valley,* it is the only one of his fictional explorations of the world about him which is free of shallow optimism. The purpose of the story—and it is tempting, though unverifiable, to read "The Blind Grandfather" as thematically autobiographical—is to examine the inevitable disillusion brought about by age and by the destruction of youthful hopes. The grandfather's life had begun auspiciously: he had known domestic bliss, which Flint constantly affirms is the only true joy; he had compensated for the loss of his wife by building a beautiful world in his mind; yet every attempt at happiness had ended in disaster. The story is in a way a retelling of the Book of Job; and, more to the point of Flint's own artistic career, it represents an inverse explanation of the resolution of *Francis Berrian* and *Arthur Clenning.* In both these novels, it will be remembered, the hero finally ends both happy and fortunate—his happiness is symbolized by his domestic relations; his good fortune, by his worldly goods. "The Blind Grandfather" begins where these two novels end; it shows a man who is both happy and fortunate, but whose happiness and good fortune are stripped away. How then is he to live?

The answer of course is found in his concluding remark to his granddaughter. The grandfather's statement represents, for all Flint's ostentatious piety and often priggish morality, one of the very few times he ever resolves a story in a truly religious way. For the story, like the Book of Job, explores the greatness of God and the inability of man to comprehend Him. In his introduction to "The Blind Grandfather" Flint mentions his reason for telling the tale. He points out that—while most people "feel nothing but their own sensations," and when they look at life cannot see beneath its surface—those "who are endowed with a contemplative mind" find that life offers "food for volumes of meditation" (250). At the end of the tale, when Flint is again aboard ship, he reflects that "amidst all the tedious babble, and heartless mirth and garrulity, it was long before I ceased to think, painfully, of the lovely Ruth and her blind grandfather" (264). What the experience told in "The Blind Grandfather" has done for Flint is to enable him to look beneath the surface of life and to get some comprehension of its meaning. The understanding Flint finally achieves, however, unlike the homiletic resolution of most of his stories, is not reducible to a didactic platitude. It is true that the story gives food for meditation, but our meditation is upon the nature of life itself—not upon some simple pious truth which may be extracted from it.

None of the stories printed in the *Knickerbocker* approaches the quality of "The Blind Grandfather." The first, a long tale which appeared in two parts in November and December of 1833, though it is almost exactly contemporaneous with "The Blind Grandfather," has none of that story's power. "The First Steamboat on the La Plata; or, 'The Monogamist,'" is another story of South American adventure. It purports to be a true experience of a man—the "Monogamist" of the title—who had taken a young relative to South America. While there, they had met the distinguished Peruvian aristocrat Balthazar de Montanos and his daughter Ines, with whom they had ascended the La Plata River on the first steamboat ever to make the trip. The

Monogamist thinks that Ines is falling in love with him, but she is really attracted to his young relative, Theodore. On a journey across the mountains the party is attacked by bandits, and Theodore distinguishes himself by leading the defense and by killing the bandit leader. Finally Theodore, predictably enough, marries Ines, not really to the displeasure of the Monogamist, a confirmed bachelor. All live happily ever after.

"The Monogamist" is a pleasant story with no fiber whatever. Its interest depends on the cliché that a girl always appears indifferent to the one she loves, and hence the Monogamist can misinterpret her apparent coldness to Theodore as affection for himself. Unfortunately this variation on the theme of mistaken identity cannot sustain our interest for the thirty-six pages of the story, and there is little else to hold our attention.[12]

"Macoupin: Or, the Talking Potato" appeared in November, 1834. It is a silly attack on Roman Catholicism which in the hands of an abler satirist could have been very effective.[13] The basic irony of the story is a clever one. Macoupin is an Indian, a great talker; he is renowned for his laziness, his ability to drink, and his way with the ladies. Since he is absolutely unable to perform any useful vocation, he naturally gravitates to the position of medicine man because, as Flint says, "preaching was his grand vocation" (IV, 373). In Macoupin's tribe are some Jesuit missionaries, one of whom is young, handsome, and pious and who becomes a rival of Macoupin. Flint tells us that the Jesuit's and Macoupin's qualifications for the priesthood are approximately the same, though the Jesuit is, if anything, better qualified and hence more successful in his chosen vocation. Macoupin is gradually supplanted by the Jesuit; and in the end of the story the Indian is swept over Niagara Falls in a canoe because he is too proud to ask his whereabouts.

Certainly this story has possibilities. The ironic comparison between the priest and the medicine man is a good one, and the fictional notion that the best qualification for the ministry is moral turpitude, with its concomitant idea that the most morally reprehensible candidate will be the most successful minister could be made the basis of a really biting satire. But Flint is unwilling or unable to develop the implications inherent in his material. We are never allowed to forget that this story is about Jesuits and Indians and not about right-thinking men of God and their pious congregations. As a result, the story—completely unintentionally on Flint's part—has a certain quality of Pharisaical smugness. One can hear Flint saying, with the Pharisee in the parable, "God, I thank thee, that I am not as other men are, extortioners, unjust, adulterers, or even as this publican"—or Indian, or Jesuit.

"Hannah Hervey," the final story in the *Knickerbocker*, appeared in March, 1836. It is nothing more than a moral homily on what was an obsessive subject with Flint in his last years: the necessity of domestic bliss to happiness. Considered as a work of art the story is a complete failure, and it is probably unjust to bring esthetic criteria to bear upon it. It is, in common with most of Flint's work, a fictional biography, and, like much of his worst writing, it has no unity other than that of temporal events. Flint tells how on a canal boat traveling from Rochester to Schenectady he had met a young man who had told him a story as they floated along. By the side of the canal, the young man says, is the house of a Mr. Morrison Hervey, an English emigrant who had married the seventh daughter of a poor English curate. The young man had met Mr. Hervey when he had gone to his house as a pupil, and had there met as well Mr. Hervey's five children. He had particularly remembered one daughter, Hannah. When a cholera epidemic had struck, all the Herveys except Hannah and her mother had died; and the young man had been so inspired by Hannah's moral qualities when she had been nursing the sick members of her family that he had mentioned her to a rich friend of his named Henderson L—. Henderson had gone with the young man to see this paragon of virtue for himself and had in turn been so impressed that he had immediately married her. The story ends with a long peroration to domestic bliss.

"Hannah Hervey" contains almost all the blemishes which mar the rest of Flint's fiction without having any of the compensating virtues of his better stories. It is sad to think that his literary career ended so badly; yet some such result was inevitable, given a man with Flint's esthetic principles. In "Hannah Hervey" we see for the last time, almost as an emblem of Flint's career as a man of letters, the artistic failure which must result when the meaning of a work of fiction is not properly wedded to its "story." With this final tale, Flint's career as a man of letters came full circle. Like the exemplum in his first published sermon, "Hannah Hervey" does not pretend to be a work of art. It is a work of morality, an exhortation, and its story serves only as a sugar coating to disguise the taste of the pill within.

CHAPTER 6

A Final Estimate

I T IS ALWAYS EASY to confuse that historical interest a writer may possess with whatever artistic merit his work may have in its own right. The assumption that a writer of admitted historic importance must be of esthetic significance as well is one to which literary historians and critics are unfortunately prone. In any assessment of Flint's work we must without question admit that he was a man of immense influence—as novelist, geographer-historian, and biographer. Whatever we think of the artistic merits of *Francis Berrian*—to take for an example the novel which the consensus of criticism has always maintained was his best—the fact that it was important as the first novel in English dealing with Texas, the fact that it established the "vogue for Hispanic backdrops," and the more significant fact that it originated the standard plot for the international subject south of the border "of the triangle of the rugged, clean-living Yankee hero, the cowardly, sensual, and corrupt Spanish American rival, and the sweet convent-bred Spanish heroine"[1] are true without question. Yet, the novel's importance granted, it does not necessarily follow that *Francis Berrian* is a book which would repay the attention of any besides professional historians of American literature.

Any attempt to revive Flint's work to general public notice must frankly admit that it has grave faults both in conception and in execution. Even Flint's contemporaries saw that his writing was often hasty and badly executed. The only bad feature of the *Condensed Geography and History*, says an otherwise highly laudatory reviewer writing in the *American Quarterly Review*, is to be found in Flint's "careless and loose phraseology" and other offenses against "*purity* of language."[2]

"To those who can not only endure, but who really like his style, he has made a useful book," one reviewer superciliously remarked of the *Lectures Upon Natural History*.[3] The reviewer for the *North American Review*, who thought highly of the *Recollections of the Last Ten Years*, felt it was nevertheless necessary to point out that "many parts of the work bear evident marks of haste in the composition."[4] Such critical comments could be indefinitely multiplied, and the modern reader is likely to agree with them. There is not a single fictional work of Flint's which can be accepted without grave esthetic reservations. Even in what in this writer's opinion is unquestionably his best novel, *The Shoshonee Valley*, there are long and tedious sections which cry for revision and which cannot successfully be explained away on the grounds of some overriding artistic purpose which in a larger context might be held to justify them.

Considered strictly on the basis of esthetic criteria, Flint's works are at best limited successes and at worst almost total failures. His novels, as I have suggested, may most successfully be interpreted as parables, but this criterion in itself implies the value judgment that they succeed in spite of their esthetic qualifications rather than because of them. Flint's omnipresent moralizing, his carelessness in writing, his awkwardly constructed plots—all are serious defects in his fiction; and a realistic appraisal of his work must admit them to be such.

Perhaps more serious than the faults which are directly chargeable to Flint's own lack of literary ability is the dated quality of most of his work. An author who devotes his career largely to historical investigation of contemporary phenomena and to the cataloguing of impermanent data must inevitably lose some of his freshness. This is especially true of the scientific writer, whose findings must in their very nature soon be superseded or modified. It is also true of the writer on divinity, who finds himself arguing problems which to the next generation are of little importance, and nonexistent to the generation following that. Finally, a man such as Flint, who believed in the dissemination of useful knowledge as one of the most important duties of literature, must reckon with the impermanence to which all useful knowledge is subject. Yesterday's practicality is today's esoterica and of interest only to the curious antiquarian.

Yet, when all is said, Flint's work cannot all be defined as of one piece and then conveniently relegated to some scholarly happy hunting ground. Though much of his writing is so dated as to be of no relevance to any but specialists, and though much as well is of such inferior quality as to interest only the historian of taste, nevertheless not all of it may justly be ignored.

Of Flint's nonfictional writing, now generally forgotten, almost all is only of limited interest or significance. His researches in science are long since buried, and should not be resurrected. Even his geographies and histories, though the reader may spend a profitable hour browsing in them, are no longer of much interest except as curiosities. The best of them is the *Recollections of the Last Ten Years*, which is a book that should be more widely known. Of all the geographies and histories, this work alone is immediately relevant to the non-specialist—and for reasons unintended by Flint. For the *Recollections*, though the factual information contained in it is no longer accurate or complete, is still one of the very best eye-witness accounts of the settlement of the West. In addition, it is one of the very few narratives which does not depend for interest on the sensational quality of the events told in it. Hand-to-hand encounters with Indians and grizzly bears form no part of it. It is rather an honest report of the trials of emigration faced by an average man. As such it is of absorbing interest to the twentieth-century reader who has been fed to satiety on the Western myth of derring-do and romantic peril. The other histories and the *Western Monthly Review* are of antiquarian interest only.

Flint's three narrations of pioneer life have fared little better than his other nonfictional work. *The Personal Narrative of James O. Pattie*—ironically, the best known and the one for which Flint was least responsible—was given a certain claim on posterity when Thwaites included it in his monumental *Early Western Travels*, and it has since been reprinted.[5] *Indian Wars of the West* is now forgotten; and the *Biographical Memoir of Daniel Boone*, "over whose charmed pages thousands of western boys have pored, as they sat by the winter fire,"[6] is now read only by scholars in somewhat more prosaic surroundings.

Very few prospective readers would lament the oblivion to which the *Indian Wars* has been consigned; but the *Biographical*

Memoir, now out of print and almost forgotten, is a real loss to American letters. Of all Flint's writing—historical or fictional—it is without question the best. Its story is compellingly told, and it alone of Flint's work is almost totally free from the blemishes which mar his other writing. Simple and direct in style, it contains no pretentious fine writing or pompous moralizing. It is the only book of his which we can read today with sheer pleasure, unalloyed with the feeling that we are doing something praiseworthy. It deserves to be better known.

The merits of Flint's fiction are harder to assess. The reader's first honest reaction to any of his imaginative writing is pretty sure to be that of disappointment. His short stories, with the exception of "Oolemba in Cincinnati" and "The Blind Grandfather," are of little merit; and even these are no better than the other now forgotten tales of the nineteenth-century periodicals. Flint's literary talent was not for the short story. He himself apparently realized this, for he wrote relatively little short fiction, concentrating instead on five novels. Two of these, *George Mason* and *The Lost Child,* are justly forgotten today. *Arthur Clenning* is a novel which is interesting—one hesitates to say profound—in intention, though poorly presented. The modern reader will find it curiously uncompelling, and an honest appraisal of its merits does not seem to warrant any concerted attempt to resuscitate it. *Francis Berrian* has long been considered Flint's best work, though critical consensus has not been unanimous.[7] In my opinion the merits in conception of this work do not counter the manifold defects in execution. It is too contrived; and, though we may perhaps speculatively agree with Flint's purposes in writing it, we cannot even speculatively accept the Mexican world he creates. With the critics of whom Martha Berrian complained in the *Western Monthly Review,* we must finally deny the story's reality.

This appraisal leaves us with Flint's last novel, *The Shoshonee Valley.* Though no one would pretend that this is the Great American Novel, one might still make a case for its very real interest. Of all Flint's novels, it has been the least noticed; but in my view it stands up best to critical scrutiny. In common with all Flint's other fiction, it shares the faults of general awkwardness of construction and of specific silliness of incident; yet at the same time it is both the most profoundly conceived and the most skillfully executed of all his novels. Unlike all his other fiction, *The Shoshonee Valley* is emotionally compelling as well as rationally intriguing; the story which Flint tells us is one we do not easily forget.

Yet Flint's best writing is not to be found in his novels, and whatever reputation he may come to possess will not depend upon his literary achievement in them. The *Recollections of the Last Ten Years* and the *Biographical Memoir of Daniel Boone* are the two volumes which without doubt deserve to exist outside the cloisters of scholarly collections. James Flint clearly saw his cousin Timothy's real merit as a writer: Not as a novelist, but as the chronicler of the peerless valley will he be remembered.

Notes and References

Chapter One

1. Though the biographical interpretations in this essay are my own, matters of fact, unless otherwise noted, are cited primarily from John Ervin Kirkpatrick's *Timothy Flint. Pioneer, Missionary, Author, Editor. 1780-1840* (Cleveland, 1911), and to a lesser extent from William H. Venable's "Timothy Flint, Missionary, Geographer, Editor, Novelist, and Poet," in his *Beginnings of Literary Culture in the Ohio Valley. Historical and Biographical Sketches* (Cincinnati, 1891), pp. 323-60.

2. *Letters from An American Farmer* (New York, 1904), p. 60 (Letter III).

3. "The Missouri Trapper," *Western Monthly Review*, I (May, 1827), 28.

4. See Lucy L. Hazard, *The Frontier in American Literature* (New York, [1927]), p. 124.

5. This, according to John Filson, is Daniel Boone's reflection upon the settlement of Kentucky. See Willard Rouse Judson, ed., *Filson's Kentucke* (Louisville, 1930), p. 50.

6. Actually, whether this memory is really Timothy's is not certain. The departure of the Ohio settlers must have been a family event of considerable importance, and Timothy's memory may be a pastiche of family gossip. Temple Cutler, son of the Manasseh Cutler who led the wagon which Timothy remembered so vividly, recalls the lettering as saying: "For the Ohio at the Muskingum." Since he was only six years old at the time, his testimony may also be questioned.

7. "Reminiscences of a Recent Journey from Cincinnati to Boston," *The Knickerbocker*, II (October, 1833), 254.

8. *Recollections of the Last Ten Years* (Boston, 1826), pp. 44-45.

9. *A Sermon Preached . . . at the Ordination of the Rev. Ebenezer Hubbard* (Newburyport, 1808), pp. 17-20.

10. "The Past—the Present—and the Future," *The Knickerbocker*, IV (September, 1834), 173.

Chapter Two

1. J. E. Kirkpatrick, *Timothy Flint*, p. 249.

2. *American Monthly Magazine*, I (April, 1829), 75; *The Athenaeum*, No. 375 (January 3, 1835), p. 12.

3. *Domestic Manners of the Americans,* II (New York, n.d.), 155.

4. "Writers of the Western Country," *Western Monthly Review,* II (June, 1828), 11-21; "Sketches of the Literature of the United States," *The Athenaeum* (1835). The editor of *The Athenaeum* has pared down Flint's already short notices of American writers by eliminating mention of many who had been covered in an earlier series of articles. Hence Flint's cursory notice of fiction and poetry is not entirely his own doing, in this series at least. Nevertheless, even had the editor of *The Athenaeum* left Flint's articles as they were, they would still have been overwhelmingly nonliterary in scope.

5. For an amusing discussion of the history of the Indian in the advertisement of patent medicines, see James Harvey Young, *The Toadstool Millionaires; A Social History of Patent Medicines in America Before Federal Regulation* (Princeton, 1961), pp. 9, 176-79, 192-93.

6. This hostility toward the reviews is by no means confined to the "Editor's Address." Most of Flint's pronouncements on American literature mention the attitude of the reviews as one of the chief obstacles toward its growth. See for example his "Impediments of American Literature," in the *Western Monthly Review,* II (February, 1829), 481-86, and his "Sketches of the Literature of the United States," *The Athenaeum,* No. 418 (October 31, 1835), pp. 817-19, though these by no means exhaust the subject.

7. Among other studies, by C. M. Lombard in "Timothy Flint: Early American Disciple of French Romanticism," *Revue de Littérature Comparée,* XXXVI (Avril-Juin, 1962), 276-82; Sister Mary Agatha Sheehan, "A Study of the First Four Novels of Texas," M. A. Thesis, Catholic University of America, Washington, D. C., 1939; Frederick S. Stimson, "'Francis Berrian': Hispanic Influence on American Romanticism," *Hispania,* XLII (December, 1959), 511-16. All rightly make a case for Flint as in some way a *Romantic.* None of these studies, however, defines just how Romanticism is operative in Flint's writing, and none is sufficiently conscious of the difficulties of definition inherent in the term *Romantic.* See Arthur O. Lovejoy, "On the Discrimination of Romanticisms," *Essays in the History of Ideas* (New York, 1955), pp. 228-53.

8. Perry Miller, in his brilliant essay "Errand Into the Wilderness," emphasizes the fact that very early in the American experience this feeling of America as a utopia which has somehow failed becomes dominant. See *Errand Into the Wilderness* (Cambridge, Massachusetts, 1956), pp. 1-15.

9. The modern reader, coming on Bellamy—far and away the most popular of the late-nineteenth-century utopian writers—for the first time, finds it difficult to re-create in his mind the profound dis-

satisfaction with the American experience and the deep-seated world-wide social discontent which supported the translation of *Looking Backward* into more than twenty languages and induced so profound a philosopher as John Dewey to list it seriously as second in influence only to Marx's *Das Kapital* of books published in the nineteenth century. Sylvia E. Bowman in *The Year 2000; A Critical Biography of Edward Bellamy* (New York, 1958) and in *Edward Bellamy Abroad; An American Prophet's Influence* (New York, 1962), has exhaustively assessed Bellamy's influence and the social conditions which gave rise to late nineteenth-century utopianism. See also Erich Fromm's perceptive foreword to the New American Library edition of *Looking Backward* (New York, 1960). It is easy for us to be condescending. We prefer our utopianism in a different form, and find nothing comical in *The Lonely Crowd* or *The Organization Man*.

10. The best study of Owenite socialism and its backgrounds may be found in Arthur Eugene Bestor, *Backwoods Utopias. The Sectarian and Owenite Phases of Communitarian Socialism in America, 1663-1829* (Philadelphia, 1950). Much has been written on the other American communitarian societies, but the best survey is still Charles Nordhoff's 1875 eye-witness account of them, *The Communistic Societies of the United States* (New York, 1961). For more particular information on the Shakers, one of the most bizarre of the sects, see Edward Andrews, *The People Called Shakers. A Search for the Perfect Society* (New York, 1953). Much has been written on Brook Farm, but a pleasant survey, which also contains a resumé of the weirdest of American communitarian notions, those of Charles Fourier, is Edith Roelker Curtis, *A Season in Utopia. The Story of Brook Farm* (New York, 1961).

11. *American Monthly Magazine,* I (April, 1829), 75; *The Athenaeum,* No. 375 (January 3, 1835), p. 12.

12. *Recollections,* p. 15; *History and Geography,* I, 157.

13. *Recollections,* pp. 52-53. This is by no means an isolated sentiment. For another example, see above, p. 61.

14. *Western Monthly Review,* I, 28; I, 118.

15. *Western Monthly Review,* I, 133-34. The fact that man is a social animal and cannot achieve either happiness or moral perfection in solitude is one of Flint's most deeply held anti-romantic beliefs. One of his novels, *The Life and Adventures of Arthur Clenning,* is almost entirely concerned with demonstrating the superiority of society to solitude.

16. Flint is, it goes without saying, correct in his appraisal. An amusing account of the fruitless search for the Wild West by later travelers may be found in Robert G. Athearn, *Westward the Briton* (New York, 1953), pp. 48-61.

17. *History and Geography,* I, 313-14; I, 287.

18. *History and Geography,* I, 396.

19. *Lectures Upon Natural History,* p. 375.

20. *Indian Wars of the West,* pp. 6-7. The development of this strange and totally unfounded notion that "rain follows the plow" has been thoroughly studied by Henry Nash Smith in *Virgin Land; The American West as Symbol and Myth* (Cambridge, Massachusetts, 1950), pp. 207-13.

21. *Lectures Upon Natural History,* p. 94.

22. *Recollections,* p. 150.

23. *Western Monthly Review,* I, 141.

24. *Recollections,* p. 144.

25. *A Condensed Geography,* I, 183.

26. *Recollections,* p. 158.

27. *History and Geography,* I, 111-12. These few comments by no means exhaust Flint's remarks about the Indians, though they do give a representative range of his opinions. For a fine general survey of nineteenth-century attitudes toward the Indian see Roy Harvey Pearce, *The Savages of America. A Study of the Indian and the Idea of Civilization* (Baltimore, 1953).

Chapter Three

1. For the indirect influence of the *Personal Narrative* upon *Francis Berrian* see below, pp. 116-118, which may as well serve to support the good faith of Flint and the at least partial veracity of Pattie.

2. "James Ohio Pattie," in *The Dictionary of American Biography.*

3. The Indian failure to unite in time against white aggression and inability to form a stable permanent alliance were undoubtedly the two major causes of their defeat. For a good modern popular history of the failure of successive Indian attempts at unity, see Alvin M. Josephy, *The Patriot Chiefs; A Chronicle of American Indian Leadership* (New York, 1961). Flint also concerns himself with the question of the inability of the Indians to organize against the whites in his short story "Oolemba in Cincinnati."

4. Though Flint is not absolutely consistent on the question of the inferiority or equality of the various "races," the overall tendency of his view supports the idea that other races are inferior to the white only insofar as they will not take up white, and more specifically American, ways. Thus Flint condemns the French *coureurs du bois* on the grounds that they have "gone native" and taken up Indian customs, a condemnation which also applies to Boone, Harrod and the rest of the frontiersmen, but from which the settler is exempt. Flint

seems to feel that racial limitations are at the bottom social limitations, and that any individual can rise above them, once he can be made to understand the rational superiority of American institutions. This is largely the point of *Francis Berrian* and to a lesser extent of *The Shoshonee Valley.*

5. See Roy Harvey Pearce on "red gifts and white gifts" in *The Savages of America,* especially pages 196-236.

6. For Filson and his work, see Willard Rouse Jillson, ed., *Filson's Kentucke* (Louisville, 1930).

7. A pirated edition of only the Appendix containing the "Adventures of Col. Daniel Boon" was printed in Norwich, Connecticut, in 1786, as *The Adventures of Colonel Daniel Boon . . . Written By . . . Himself.* This edition, much abridged and with a very corrupt text, was printed together with an account of Indian captivity, and was obviously intended to capitalize on the sensationalism of the events recounted in both narratives. For discussions of the "captivity narrative" as a genre, see Phillips D. Carleton, "The Indian Captivity," *AL,* XV (May, 1943), 169-80, who pleads for their analysis on literary and esthetic rather than on purely historical grounds and, more important, Roy Harvey Pearce, "The Significances of the Captivity Narrative," *AL,* XIX (March, 1947), 1-20, who makes a very interesting case for the captivity narrative as the cheap escape fiction of the early nineteenth century.

8. Jillson's remark that Filson "saved Boone from an oblivion that has all but swallowed up Harrod and many others" (*Kentucke,* p. 142) is undoubtedly true insofar as Filson's *Kentucke* set the precedent for later writers to use Boone's biography as the epitome of the pioneer way of life. Nevertheless, Henry Nash Smith is right in his suggestion that Flint's biography of Boone became "the most widely read book about a Western character published during the first half of the nineteenth century" (*Virgin Land,* p. 55).

9. *Indian Wars of the West,* pp. 223-24.

10. See *Indian Wars of the West,* pp. 54-55, 219, 221-22. The fact that Flint mentions a personal acquaintance with Boone only relatively late in his life, and after Boone had died, has caused some to doubt his claim. There seems, however, no valid reason to assume Flint was not telling the truth.

11. I have suggested above that the *Recollections* detail Flint's own identification with the West, and his final renunciation of New England, as seen in his personal decision to return West to live in 1825. His own identification with the West is basic to his literary exploration of Western history, and his interest in the pioneers. As late as 1822, it will be recalled, Flint still thought of himself as an exiled Yankee.

12. Flint wrote only a few poems, none of which is, in my opinion, of enough merit or interest to warrant discussion. A complete list may be found in Kirkpatrick, *Timothy Flint*, p. 313. Kirkpatrick also reprints one poem, "The Being of a God," pp. 302-3.

13. The absolute sexual morality of the Indians is an article of faith with Flint, who ascribes it at various times to their lack of passion or, as in *The Shoshonee Valley*, to a certain moral decency.

14. Henry Nash Smith, in *Virgin Land*, pp. 55-56, has noted, on the basis of this passage, what he considers an inconsistency in Flint's treatment of Boone. The inconsistency can be resolved, it seems to me, by considering the "evil" of civilization not as opposed to the "good" of Boone's more primitive way of life, from which it must follow that Boone's view of civilization as a good is inconsistent; rather a hierarchy of values is implied, where the "goodness" of the primitive way of life is superseded not by the evil but by the greater good of civilization. The reader should note as well the similarity of the motives which Flint attributes to Boone with those which Filson attributes to him.

15. Flint's view, at least, was that the historic Boone was the model for Natty Bumppo. See *Biographical Memoir*, p. 250.

16. Modern scholars tend to view Cooper's ultimate decision as in favor of civilization. The most persuasive statement of this case is, in my opinion, that of Roy Harvey Pearce in *The Savages of America*, especially pp. 200-12. I am not convinced.

17. *The Complete Works of James Fenimore Cooper*, V (New York, n. d. [The Leather-Stocking Edition]), 232. Such passages are legion in all the Leatherstocking Tales.

18. *Western Monthly Review*, I (September, 1827), 308.

19. *Western Monthly Review*, I (February, 1828), 606. These remarks apply specifically to *The Red Rover*.

Chapter Four

1. J. E. Kirkpatrick, *Timothy Flint*, p. 250. These remarks refer specifically to *George Mason*.

2. This aspect of the story has been perhaps too thoroughly explored by Sister Mary Agatha Sheehan, in "A Study of the First Four Novels of Texas," pp. 62-89.

3. Sister Mary Agatha Sheehan is the most vociferous critic of Flint's anti-Catholicism. That *Francis Berrian* is not anti-Catholic may be seen in Berrian's own statement that "I deem good people to be all of one religion. . . . There is enough that is common to every form of Christian faith and profession, to unite us in deeds of beneficence

and feelings of charity" (II, 254). This may represent woolly thinking, but it is not anti-Catholic; it is *anti-clerical*. Flint's objection to Catholicism is to the temporal power of the Church, which he thinks is often misused; if, however, one wishes to be a believing Catholic, that is his own affair. Berrian's refusal to attempt the conversion of either his wife or her family should make this point perfectly clear.

4. Italics in this and the following direct or paraphrased quotations from Pattie's *Personal Narrative* are mine; they are used to indicate points of more than coincidental similarity between it and *Francis Berrian*.

5. Flint uses a similar device in a humorous way in order to advertise *Francis Berrian*. He prints in the *Western Monthly Review*, I, 29-31, a letter to himself which purports to come from Martha Berrian, who deplores the fact that the reviewers—like Bishop Berkeley, to whom she compares them—refuse to take *Francis Berrian* seriously because they deny both her and her husband's existence.

6. It should be remarked, especially in light of constant critical appraisals of Flint's Romanticism, that in one sense of the term at least this attitude is completely "anti-romantic."

7. This aspect of the story closely parallels Flint's almost exactly contemporary short story in the *Western Monthly Review*, "Agnes Sorel de Merivanne: The Recluse Coquette."

8. This is part of the beginning scene of Ernest Hemingway's "Hills Like White Elephants."

9. Mr. Mason's biography, it will be perceived, bears more than a casual resemblance to Flint's own.

10. The novel was first discussed by John A. Hamilton, "Timothy Flint's 'Lost Novel,'" *AL*, XXII (March, 1950), 54-56. Hamilton describes in some detail the history of his discovery of the novel. He located through the Union Catalogue only two copies, one in the Newberry Library, Chicago, and the other in the Library of the University of Michigan. In addition, he himself located a copy in the Library of Marietta College, Marietta, Ohio. I located a fourth copy in the Yale University Library. Though other copies doubtless exist, they are generally unknown, and the book is very rare.

11. By the date of the appearance of *The Shoshonee Valley*, three of the five Leatherstocking Tales had appeared. These were: *The Pioneers* (1823); *The Last of the Mohicans* (1826); and *The Prairie* (1827).

12. Whether Flint's sympathy in these two works indicates a personal belief in the validity of Indian ways, or whether it is purely an esthetic device, I am unable finally to say. My own opinion is that Flint is here treating the Indians symbolically, much as he treated the

symbol of America in *Francis Berrian* and *Arthur Clenning*. In the text of this study I have tried to present all the evidence impartially, and the reader must judge for himself, if he wishes to do so, just where Flint's personal sympathies lie.

13. Whether Flint himself believed in the existence of a tribe of "white" Indians who lived somewhere in the fastnesses of the Rockies is uncertain. He vouches for the truth of the book in the introduction to it, though this may well be an editorial ploy; on the other hand, he subtitles the book "A Romance," which in the literary terminology of his time implies that, though the story may be "true" in a philosophical sense, it is not necessarily factual in a historical one. The notion of the Indians as in some way connected with European civilization, however, had a long and vigorous history. They were assumed quite early to be descendants of the "lost tribes" of Israel, and later their European origins were variously postulated. John Filson, for example, seriously advances the notion that somewhere to the west is a tribe of white Indians descended from the Welsh leader Madoc, who supposedly founded a colony in America in 1170. (See *Kentucke*, pp. 95-98.)

Chapter Five

1. A review of *The Bachelor Reclaimed*, printed in the New York *Commercial* and later in the Cincinnati *Mirror*, III (1834), 444. My own citation is taken from some of the papers of J. E. Kirkpatrick in the Yale University Library.

2. *The Athenaeum*, No. 402 (July 11, 1835), p. 527.

3. "Impediments of American Literature," *Western Monthly Review*, II (February, 1829), 485-86.

4. *The Athenaeum*, No. 405, p. 584.

5. *Western Monthly Review*, I (October, 1827), 338.

6. "Writers of the Western Country," *Western Monthly Review*, II (June, 1828), 13.

7. *The Athenaeum*, No. 402, p. 526.

8. See *The Athenaeum*, No. 405, pp. 584-86.

9. "The Past—the Present—and the Future," *Knickerbocker*, IV (September, 1834), 173-74.

10. IV (July, 1834), 78.

11. Preface to *The Bachelor Reclaimed*, p. v.

12. All Flint's South American stories are printed in the *Knickerbocker* at approximately the same time. "The First Steamboat on the La Plata" appears in November and December of 1833; "A Chapter in the Life of a Bachelor" in January, 1834; "Martha; or, The Grand Cataract of Bogota," a revised version of "Paulina, Or, the Cataract of Tequendama" in July, 1835.

13. Flint was proud of his satirical gift, but the modern reader is unlikely to share his self-admiration. He was also to reprint "Violetta and Thoroughgrabb" in the *Knickerbocker* for September, 1835.

Chapter Six

1. Frederick S. Stimson, "'Francis Berrian': Hispanic Influence on American Romanticism," *Hispania*, XLII (December, 1959), 513.

2. V (June, 1829), 358. The italics are the reviewer's.

3. *American Monthly Review*, III (April, 1833), 265.

4. XXIII (October, 1826), 368.

5. A recent edition (Philadelphia, 1962) with an introduction by William H. Goetzmann is now in print.

6. William H. Venable, *Literary Culture in the Ohio Valley*, p. 359.

7. Sister Mary Agatha Sheehan, *op. cit.*, has been the most perceptive modern critic to point out the book's faults.

Selected Bibliography

PRIMARY SOURCES

In this bibliography I have included only those articles in the Western Monthly Review and the Knickerbocker which I have discussed in the text of this study. Citations to books are to first editions. Occasionally I have used for a working text an edition other than the first; when this is the case I have indicated the edition used by square brackets following the citation to the first edition.

The Art of Being Happy: From the French of Droz, 'Sur L'Art D'Etre Heureux'; In A Series of Letters from a Father to his Children: With Comments and Observations. Boston: Carter and Hendee, 1832.

The Bachelor Reclaimed or Celibacy Vanquished, from the French. Philadelphia: Key & Biddle, 1834.

Biographical Memoir of Daniel Boone, the First Settler of Kentucky. Interspersed with Incidents in the Early Annals of the Country. Cincinnati: N. & G. Guilford, 1833. [Cincinnati: George Condin, 1842.] This book was published in many editions, under various titles, between 1833 and 1868. The most common variant title is *The First White Man of the West.*

"The Blind Grandfather," *The Token and Atlantic Souvenir. A Christmas and New Year's Present.* Boston: Gray and Bowen, 1833, pp. 250-64.

A Condensed Geography and History of the Western States, or the Mississippi Valley. 2 vols. Cincinnati: E. H. Flint, 1828.

Francis Berrian, or the Mexican Patriot. 2 vols. Boston: Cummings, Hilliard, and Co., 1826.

George Mason, the Young Backwoodsman; or "Don't Give Up the Ship." A Story of the Mississippi. Boston: Hilliard, Gray, Little, and Wilkins, 1829.

The History and Geography of the Mississippi Valley. To Which Is Appended a Condensed Physical Geography of the Atlantic United States, and the Whole American Continent. 2 vols. Cincinnati: E. H. Flint, 1832 [Boston: Carter, Hendee, and Co., 1833. 2 vols. in 1 vol.].

Indian Wars of the West; Containing Biographical Sketches of Those Pioneers Who Headed the Western Settlers in Repelling the

Attacks of the Savages, Together With A View of the Character, Manners, Monuments, and Antiquities of the Western Indians. Cincinnati: E. H. Flint, 1833.

The Knickerbocker:

"Obstacles to American Literature," II (September, 1833), 161-70.

"Reminiscenses of a Recent Journey from Cincinnati to Boston," II (October, 1833), 242-63.

"The First Steamboat on the La Plata; or, 'The Monogamist,'" II (November, 1833), 321-40; (December, 1833), 433-50.

"A Chapter in the Life of a Bachelor, A South American Story," III (January, 1834), 6-15.

"The Past, the Present and the Future," IV (September, 1834), 165-75.

"Macoupin: Or, the Talking Potato," IV (November, 1834), 372-77.

"Martha; Or, the Grand Cataract of Bogota," VI (July, 1835), 28-43. A slightly revised version of "Paulina, Or, the Cataract of Tequendama," which appeared earlier in the *Western Monthly Review.*

"Hannah Hervey," VII (March, 1836), 251-61.

Lectures Upon Natural History, Geology, Chemistry, the Application of Steam, and Interesting Discoveries in the Arts. Boston: Lilly, Wait, Colman, and Holden; Cincinnati: E. H. Flint, 1833.

The Life and Adventures of Arthur Clenning. 2 vols. Philadelphia: Towar & Hogan, 1828.

The Lost Child. Boston: Carter & Hendee, and Putnam & Hunt, 1830.

"Oolemba in Cincinnati," in James Hall, ed., *The Western Souvenir, A Christmas and New Year's Gift for 1829,* Cincinnati: N. and G. Guilford, 1829, pp. 68-101.

The Personal Narrative of James O. Pattie, of Kentucky. Cincinnati: J. H. Wood, 1831. [In Reuben Gold Thwaites, ed., *Early Western Travels, 1748-1846,* XVIII, Cleveland: The Arthur H. Clark Company, 1905, pp. 25-324.] Until recently the Thwaites edition was the only modern edition of Pattie's *Narrative.* It is still the most accessible in libraries, though out of print. A new edition, edited by William H. Goetzmann (Philadelphia: Lippincott, 1962), is now readily obtainable.

Recollections of the Last Ten Years, Passed in Occasional Residences and Journeyings in the Valley of the Mississippi, From Pittsburg [sic] and the Missouri to the Gulf of Mexico, and From Florida to the Spanish Frontier; In a Series of Letters to the Rev. James Flint, of Salem, Massachusetts. Boston: Cummings, Hilliard, and Company, 1826.

A Sermon Delivered in Leominster, at the Commencement of the Year, Lord's Day, January 1st, 1815. Leicester, Massachusetts: Hori Brown, 1815.

A Sermon Preached May 11, 1802 at the Ordination of the Rev. Ebenezer Hubbard, Over the Second Church and Society in Newbury. Newburyport: E. W. Allen, 1808. A proof error in the title misdates this sermon May 11, 1802; it should read May 11, 1808.

The Shoshonee Valley; a Romance. 2 vols. Cincinnati: E. H. Flint, 1830.

"Sketches of the Literature of the United States," *The Athenaeum*, No. 401 (July 4, 1835), pp. 511-12; No. 402 (July 11, 1835), pp. 526-27; No. 405 (August 1, 1835), pp. 584-86; No. 407 (August 15, 1835), pp. 624-25; No. 409 (August 29, 1835), pp. 666-68; No. 411 (September 12, 1835), pp. 696-98; No. 412 (September 19, 1835), pp. 714-16; No. 416 (October 17, 1835), pp. 782-83; No. 417 (October 24, 1835), pp. 802-3; No. 418 (October 31, 1835), pp. 817-19; No. 419 (November 7, 1835), pp. 831-32.

The Western Monthly Review:

"Advertisement to the First Volume of the Western Monthly Review," I (May, 1827), iii-v.

"Editor's Address," I (May, 1827), 9-20.

"The Lost Child," I (May, 1827), 20-23.

"The Missouri Trapper," I (May, 1827), 27-28.

"Correspondence," I (May, 1827), 29-31. This letter Flint wrote to himself but it supposedly comes from Martha Miguela Berrian.

"Canals," I (June, 1827), 73-78.

"New Views of Society . . . by Robert Owen," I (June, 1827), 105-18. An expanded review of Owen's writing and career.

"National Character of the Western People," I (July, 1827), 133-39.

"Sketches of the Character of the North American Savages," I (July, 1827), 139-42.

"Boon's [sic] Remembrances of Arriving in Kentucky," I (July, 1827), 154. A poem.

"Extracts from the Gazette of Oregon, Mouth of Columbia, July 5, 1900," I (September, 1827), 255-63.

"To Correspondents," I (September, 1827), 308-10. Remarks on James Fenimore Cooper.

"Newspapers," I (October, 1827), 335-39.

"Jemima O'Keefy.—A Sentimental Tale," I (November, 1827), 384-93.

"Violetta and Thoroughgrabb. A Tale," I (December, 1827), 442-53. Reprinted, slightly changed, under the same title in the *Knickerbocker*, VI (September, 1835), 173-86.

"The Hermit of the Prairies," I (February, 1828), 569-86.

"The Red Rover," I (February, 1828), 603-8. A review.

"Writers of the Western Country," II (June, 1828), 11-21.

"Novels," II (December, 1828), 419-20. This prefaces an excerpt from *The Shoshonee Valley*.

"Report of Mr. Judah . . . relative to the Wabash and Miami Canal," II (January, 1829), 459-60. A review.

"Impediments of American Literature," II (February, 1829), 481-86.

"Ewing's Report . . . Relative to the Wabash and Miami Canal," II (May, 1829), 701. A review.

"Agnes Sorel de Merivanne: The Recluse Coquette," III (August, 1829), 57-67.

"*Sketches of American Character*, By Mrs. Sarah J. Hale . . . ," III (January, 1830), 375-77. A review.

"Paulina, Or The Cataract of Tequendama," III (March, 1830), 462-69.

SECONDARY SOURCES

This list of scholarly studies is primarily, though not exclusively, confined to twentieth-century commentaries. Since an exhaustive listing of earlier studies may be found in Kirkpatrick's biography of Flint, it seemed pointless to list them here. With few exceptions, studies which contain no particular reference to Flint, however useful they may be as background material, have been eliminated, even though many have been alluded to in the text of this essay or mentioned briefly in the notes. The list of reviews does not pretend to be exhaustive. It is a subjective listing, containing those reviews which to my mind give a representative range of contemporary opinion of Flint and his work. Other reviews are listed in Kirkpatrick's biography, where the interested reader may find them.

A. *Books and Articles.*

BRYAN, DANIEL. *The Mountain Muse: Comprising the Adventures of Daniel Boone; And the Power of Virtuous and Refined Beauty.* Harrisonburg, Virginia: Davidson & Bourne, 1813. This long narrative poem is the most important fictional predecessor of Flint's *Biographical Memoir of Daniel Boone.*

CARLETON, PHILLIPS D. "The Indian Captivity," *American Literature,*

XV (May, 1943), 169-80. Draws attention to the literary aspects of the narratives of Indian captivity.

FILSON, JOHN. *The Discovery, Settlement and Present State of Kentucke*. Wilmington: James Adams, 1784. The most important historical source for Flint's *Biographical Memoir of Daniel Boone*. The definitive modern edition, to which references in the text of this study refer, is Willard Rouse Judson, ed., *Filson's Kentucke*. Louisville: John Procton & Co., 1930. This edition contains a facsimile of Filson's 1784 text with annotations, and a biographical and critical sketch of his life and work.

[————]. *The Adventures of Colonel Daniel Boon, One of the First Settlers at Kentucke: . . . Written By the Colonel Himself. To Which Are Added, A Narrative of the Captivity, And Extraordinary Escape of Mrs. Francis Scott . . .* Norwich, Connecticut: John Trumbull, 1786. One of the most interesting of the many pirated editions of Filson's work. Corrupt in text, it was obviously intended to capitalize on the sensationalism of the events recounted and, possibly to aid in sales, the title page indicates—falsely—that Boone himself wrote the work. It is likely, though unverifiable, that this edition of *Kentucke* is the first with which Flint was acquainted.

HAMILTON, JOHN A. "Timothy Flint's 'Lost Novel,'" *American Literature*, XXII (March, 1950), 54-56. Recounts the author's discovery of three copies of *The Lost Child*.

KIRKPATRICK, JOHN ERVIN. *Timothy Flint. Pioneer, Missionary, Author, Editor. 1780-1840.* Cleveland: The Arthur H. Clark Company, 1911. The definitive biography of Flint. Contains a valuable, though on occasion slightly inaccurate, bibliography of Flint's writings and nineteenth-century studies of him.

LOMBARD, C. A. "Timothy Flint: Early American Disciple of French Romanticism," *Revue de Littérature Comparée*, XXXVI (Avril-Juin, 1962), 276-82. Traces the influence of French Romanticism, especially the works of Chateaubriand and Lamartine, on Flint's writing.

MORRIS, ROBERT L. "Three Arkansas Travelers," *Arkansas Historical Quarterly*, IV (Autumn, 1945), 215-30. A survey of the opinions of Flint, Washington Irving, and the German writer Friedrich Gerstaecker about the lower Mississippi Valley, through which all three, at various times, traveled.

PEARCE, ROY HARVEY. *The Savages of America. A Study of the Indian and the Idea of Civilization.* Baltimore: The Johns Hopkins Press, 1953. A brilliant study of American attitudes toward the Indian. Indispensable for anyone interested in Indian history or in American intellectual history in general.

————. "The Significances of the Captivity Narrative," *American Literature*, XIX (March, 1947), 1-20. Studies the literary significance of the stories of Indian captivity in terms of the nature of their contemporary appeal. Thought-provoking in implication.

SEELYE, JOHN D. "Timothy Flint's 'Wicked River' and *The Confidence-Man*," *Publications of the Modern Language Association*, LXXVIII (March, 1963), 75-79. A convincing, though admittedly inferential, case for Flint's influence on Melville, especially of Flint's descriptions of the Mississippi River on *The Confidence-Man*.

SHEEHAN, SISTER MARY AGATHA. "A Study of the First Four Novels of Texas." M. A. thesis, Catholic University of America, Washington, D. C., 1939, pp. 62-89. An alternately perceptive and irritating study of *Francis Berrian*. Negative in approach, Sister Mary Agatha points out the manifold weaknesses in the novel and is highly critical of Flint's supposed anti-Catholicism.

SMITH, HENRY NASH. *Virgin Land; The American West as Symbol and Myth*. Cambridge, Massachusetts: Harvard University Press, 1950. The classic study of the West in the American imagination. Useful generally as background, and with particular reference to Flint as well.

STIMSON, FREDERICK S. " 'Francis Berrian': Hispanic Influence on American Romanticism," *Hispanica*, XLII (December, 1959), 511-16. A fine critical study of *Francis Berrian* which mentions both its importance to the later development of the "Western" and its real literary value.

TROLLOPE, MRS. FRANCES. *Domestic Manners of the Americans*. 2 vols. New York: Dodd, Mead, and Company, n. d. Interesting for her comments on Flint and his writing. She is almost embarrassingly fulsome in her praise both of him and of his work.

TURNER, ARLIN. "James Kirke Paulding and Timothy Flint," *Mississippi Valley Historical Review*, XXXIV (June, 1947), 105-11. Traces the impact of Flint's work on Paulding's, especially of the *Condensed Geography* and the *Recollections* on *Westward Ho!*

VENABLE, WILLIAM H. *Beginnings of Literary Culture in the Ohio Valley. Historical and Biographical Sketches*. Cincinnati: Robert Clarke & Co., 1891, pp. 323-60. Best short biography of Flint.

WALKER, LENNIE MERLE. "Picturesque New Mexico Revealed in Novel as Early as 1826," *New Mexico Historical Review*, XIII (July, 1938), 325-28. A short notice of *Francis Berrian* written for New Mexico "buffs," which points out that Flint's knowledge of New Mexico geography is inaccurate.

B. *Reviews*

American Monthly Magazine, I (April, 1829), 75. A short notice of the
 Western Monthly Review by N. P. Willis, always a staunch
 friend and booster of Flint.

American Monthly Review, III (April, 1833), 261-67. Review of
 Lectures Upon Natural History.

American Quarterly Review, V (June, 1829), 343-58. Review of
 Condensed Geography and History of the Western States.

Athenaeum, No. 375 (January 3, 1835), pp. 9-13. A short notice of
 Flint as part of a longer article, "Literature of the Nineteenth
 Century. America," by N. P. Willis.

Knickerbocker, I (March, 1833), 193-94. Review of *Lectures Upon
 Natural History.*

————. IV (July, 1834), 78. Review of *The Bachelor Reclaimed.*

North American Review, XXIII (October, 1826), 355-68. Review of
 Recollections of the Last Ten Years.

Quarterly Review, XLVIII (October, 1832), 201-22. A very favorable
 English review of the *Recollections of the Last Ten Years.*

Southern Review, II (August, 1828), 192-216. A favorable review of
 the *Recollections;* praises Flint particularly for his views on
 slavery and on the Indians.

United States Review and Literary Gazette, I (November, 1826),
 94-98. Early, unfavorable review of *Francis Berrian.*

Western Monthly Magazine, I (June, 1833), 262-73. A vitriolic review
 of the *Lectures Upon Natural History* by James Hall, Flint's
 colleague and none too friendly literary rival in Cincinnati.

Index

Index

"Agnes Sorel de Merivanne," 67, 68
Art of Being Happy, The, 29, 157-
58
Arthur Clenning, 29, 33-34, 118-30,
131, 133, 140, 159, 161-62, 169
Astoria, see Irving, Washington
Athenaeum, The, 48-49, 73, 151

Bachelor Reclaimed, The, 29, 67,
157, 158-60
*Biographical Memoir of Daniel
Boone*, 30, 49, 81, 87-104, 106,
168-69, 170
"Blind Grandfather, The," 160-62,
169
Boone, Daniel, 18, 82-83, 86-104
"Boon's Remembrances of Arriving
in Kentucky," 94
Bryan, Daniel, 90-93, 98
Bullard, Judge Henry Adams, 45-
46, 81, 115-16, 117-18

"Chapter in the Life of a Bachelor,
A," 159-60
Chaucer, Geoffrey, 35
Cincinnati, Ohio, 20, 40, 41, 42, 46,
49, 50, 53-54, 57, 60, 82, 97, 98,
138
*Condensed Geography and History
of the Western States, A*, 49, 54-
56, 58, 166
Cooper, James Fenimore, 102-4,
106, 119, 136-37, 139, 145, 153
Crèvecoeur, Michel Guillaume Jean
de (J. Hector St. John), 18
Criticism, *see* Literary criticism

Emerson, Ralph Waldo, 62-63
Emigration, in Flint's writing, 54-
55, 57-61, 100-1, 108-9, 114-16,
131-33

"Extracts from the Gazette of
Oregon," 68-71

Filson, John, 19, 87-93, 94, 98, 101
"First Steamboat on the La Plata,
The," 162-63
Flint, Hezekiah, and settlement of
Ohio, 19-20
Flint, James, 20, 21, 24, 33, 46-47,
48, 49, 50, 118, 170
Flint, Timothy: early life, 19-21;
attitudes toward ministry, 20-21,
23, 24, 26, 27-28, 39, 42-44;
religious career, 21-28; attitudes
toward religion, 22-25, 28-33, 42-
44; importance of religious career
to literary career, 28-38; attitudes
toward literature, 28-38; religious
training and literary style, 31-38,
51-52; missionary work, 38-45;
later life, 45-47; for writings see
specific titles
Francis Berrian, 29, 33-34, 37, 45,
46, 48, 68, 105, 107-18, 119, 120,
124-25, 127-28, 130, 133, 159,
161-62, 166, 169
Frontiersmen, 18-19, 30, 40-41, 42,
52-53, 72, 73-77, 79, 81-104, 116-
18, 140

George Mason, 27-28, 29, 36-38, 70,
107, 131-33, 135, 159, 169

"Hannah Hervey," 164-65
Harrod, James, 18, 86-87
Harvard College, 20, 45, 108, 115
Hemingway, Ernest, 37, 93, 130
"Hermit of the Prairies, The," 65-
66, 67
History and Geography of the

Date Due